GO ASK YOUR DAD

BROUGHT TO YOU BY;

Dominick Domasky Creator and Co-author of The Unofficial Guide to Fatherhood

&

Doug Lauffer OM, MA, MSci Co-author of The Unofficial Guide to Fatherhood

CONTRIBUTING AUTHORS

Al Latronica, Anthony Fludd Sr., Bill Viola Jr., Brian P. Swift, Dr. Chris Reber, Darnell Johnson, Dennis Newton, Dominick Domasky, Doug Lauffer, Dr. Edward L. Kropf Jr., Dr. Fred Simkovsky, Howard Upton, Jeff Jackson, Jesse Foster, Joe Walko, Lispert Dowdell, Mark Carney, Nigel Brown, Dr. Patrick Kelly, Reece Anderson, Shon Owens, Tommy Jones

Copyright © 2016 by Motivation Champs Publishing
Printed and Electronic Versions
ISBN-13: 978-0692688144 (Motivation Champs)
ISBN-10: 0692688145

978-0692688144

0692688145

The book was printed in the United States of America.

To order additional copies of this book, contact:
Motivation Champs Publishing, (412) 527-2213
http://motivationchamps.com/contact
www.motivationchamps.com
Or You May,
Contact one of the Book's Authors whose contact information is at the end of each of their respective chapters.

Table of Contents

This book is dedicated to all the mothers, fathers, teachers, coaches, caregivers and so many others who made sacrifices little and big for the authors of **Go Ask Your Dad**.

Thank you for your encouragement, much-needed discipline, inspiration and most of all, your unconditional love. –

The Authors of **Go Ask Your Dad**

Forward By Dominick Domasky and Doug Lauffer

If you look into any father's soul you'll find it holds a unique and heartfelt story of how deeply fatherhood has touched them. Our children may have different names, faces, strengths, and afflictions; our stories may have different protagonists and antagonists, but the challenges we fathers face are so similar that they must be shared. Every father faces highs and lows, heartbreaks and hardships, but no matter the obstacle, we must realize fatherhood is a privilege. The story of a great father starts with love—an unconditional love between father and child. If we study this story, learn from each other's pain and promise, learn from the men who love the way we love and hurt the way we hurt, won't we be more prepared?

Two years ago, I began a mission to write a book about fatherhood; however I knew that alone, I was ill-equipped for the task. I needed help, support, wisdom, and guidance, so the question was, "To whom should I turn?" I was at a loss until I recalled the words mothers had been suggesting for years: *Go Ask Your Dad*. So, I did, in fact I went and asked eight dads to share the lessons their father and fatherhood had taught them and together we created *The Unofficial Guide to Fatherhood*. I am keenly aware that the undertaking is not complete. There are more questions, and *Go Ask Your Dad* has more answers. Other fathers have messages of hope that need to be shared and *Go Ask Your Dad* helps those voices be heard. Fathers need every tool possible to ease doubts and answer questions, and this book accepts that challenge.

Fatherhood is a riddle because the answer one day is not the same the next; what works with one child may traumatize another, and while you are blessed to have eternal life, your story is not written by you alone. As proud men we can all claim we are excellent fathers; however, the proof is in the generation we created and raised.

The generation we have created will face many challenges we never knew; pregnancy pacts, gang violence, school shootings, terrorism, Common Core Math, Facebook, Snapchat, Instagram, Twitter, Periscope and more. Our children are glued to technology and they are connected 24/7. You'll hear mom say, *Go Ask Your Dad,* and newer terms like cyber-bullying, cyber school, cyber space, sexting and texting and you will want to hide.

You are up for the challenge. You need to know that you don't have to do it alone. In this book, twenty-two men from around the globe answer questions and share their fatherly insights. This book is meant to be read, one story at a time, for thirty straight days. Our hope is that you'll find knowledge, answers, and encouragement.

Our promise to you is a book filled with fatherly passion and wisdom. The men of this book are honored you would consider reading their stories and allowing them to share the wisdom they have gained. These writers take great pride in their commitment to family, fatherhood, and also great fulfillment in the personal stories they have shared. We feel it's our responsibility to pass on our stories and we offer you a guarantee: If you implement any of the lessons shared in this book, you will be on the road to becoming a better father.

Good Luck and Godspeed, Dominick Domasky and Doug Lauffer

Preface

In this book, you will find many touching stories emphasizing the importance of fatherhood. Before reading these personal accounts here are some alarming statistics to consider:

- Children in father-absent homes are almost four times more likely to be poor. In 2011, 12 percent of children in married-couple families were living in poverty, compared to 44 percent of children in mother-only families.

- 43% of US children live in homes without their father [US Department of Census] 2014

- 71% of pregnant teenagers lack a father. [US Department of Health and Human Services press release, Friday, March 26, 1999]

- 71% of high school dropouts come from fatherless homes. [National Principals Association Report on the State of High Schools

- Even after ascertaining income levels, youths in father-absent households still had significantly higher odds of incarceration than those in mother-father families. Youths who never had a father in the household experienced the highest odds. [Harper, Cynthia C. and Sara S. McLanahan. "Father Absence and Youth Incarceration." Journal of Research on Adolescence 14 September 2004: 369-397.]

Go Ask Your Dad

Chapter 1

Is Time on Your Side?
By Mark Carney

Being asked to contribute to a book celebrating being a dad is a humbling thing. I don't know if I ever will master this thing called "Fatherhood" nor is it easy to attempt to whittle the past two decades to a single lesson learned or passed on. It has given me the opportunity to reflect on the impact my dad had on my life—my parenting style—and the kind of relationship I have with each of my own boys.

As I racked my brain to sort out what I could possibly share that might in any way be construed as a life lesson to share...or some sage advice that would be in any manner viewed as insightful...I kept coming back to the notion that as much as I have gathered experience and maybe picked up a lesson or two to pass on...my boys have taught me as much about myself as I have shared with them. After all—it's impossible to wear the title of "Dad" without having a child—so it is a symbiotic dynamic that both pushes and pulls us along the path of this journey we call "Fatherhood".

But at the end of all the thinking—the brain cramps to put to paper—the questioning of my own credentials to even be included in this book—I was continuously returning to the concept of TIME. Time is of course the most precious asset we have in this world. My wife and the mother of my boys courageously battled a rare type of cancer for the better part of a decade before she passed away in November of 2012. She lived each day to its fullest...and cancer didn't win because she never quit. But it was her diagnosis that I will say gave me the gift of really being able to appreciate the present—the present of TIME.

Many of us—yes including me—tend to go through life as if tomorrow is a certainty. That sense of "we will get to it later". Or, "Ask me tomorrow". This manifests itself with how we interact with our loved ones—especially our kids. We often assume that our things at end—our day to day chores—our work we bring home—whatever—is the most absolutely critical thing that has to get done right at that moment. It is usually at the expense of our kids. Expense is a key word here—because we all choose where or with whom—we spend our time. We control this investment or lack of at times.

So before my wife was diagnosed and given a few months to live...that was way too often my world. I was wired on being the top Salesman at the search firm I was blessed to work at—I was determined to grow a new practice within that firm—I thought that by being able to buy more things for my family that I was actually giving them more. The reality was that as I worked often past seven during the week—as I went in on Saturday and Sunday mornings for a few hours—as I made the calls and sent the emails after getting home in the evening...I was in reality giving my family much less. I was robbing them and myself of TIME together.

My kids didn't care what kind of new car daddy drove—they didn't care if we had the latest flat-screen HDTV—they didn't care if we had front row seats for the next big game. But they did want to simply sit down on the old hardwood floors—crumbs and all—and pull out the Thomas the Train/Brio sets and together make a world of wooden stations and bridges and tunnels with their dad. We would go under the dining room table—zigzag through the chair legs—around corner flower stands—and up and over lamp stands. We would literally create a world that we controlled—as my wife continued her fight with cancer having that control I figured out later was a small way for us to have a sense that everything could be OK.

The little boy waited patiently for the sign from his catcher...he kicked at the worn out patch of grass in the backyard as he came set.

He brought his hands up over his head and went into his windup...fastball...of course the only pitch his catcher would ever call for the ten year old lefty to throw...and then he let it rip. Another strike..."Great Pitch Son"...his catcher called out as he stood to throw the ball back again. "Thanks Dad..." The little would boy would look in again for the sign...and the whole scene would unfold again—and again—and again—a pitchcount of around sixty pitches or so every other day—in the spring—summer and fall. The catcher even invested in his own genuine Sears and Roebuck catcher's mitt even though his son was a lefty and could never use it in a game. This was our time.

TIME—those pitching sessions in my back yard where my dad took many a shorthops of his shins in relation to strikes as I learned to throw consistently are some of the best days I spent in my life. When I had the opportunity to coach my own boys in soccer—then baseball—and then basketball it was a great way to make an investment in their life. Sports is not the answer for everything I recognize and acknowledge that...but it provided so many one on one moments with each of my boys that I wouldn't trade for anything and I sometimes wish I could return to.

The early morning drives to the office on the weekends were gradually replaced by early morning trips to the batting cages at the field. "Getting our work in" became a time to grab a bucket or two of balls—share a big bag of Sunflower seeds—and just be able to forget about whatever else had happened that week or that we didn't want to admit could happen with the next scan or test result for my wife/their mom. Sitting on a bucket—with a bucket of balls in front of me—spitting seeds—as fog still lingered over the diamonds in the complex all around us it was literally just a boy and his dad.

The games that followed over the years were always great—as a coach I really was blessed to see so many fine young kids grow up right in front of me—but it is those one on one sessions—buckets in the batting cage...catching them in the backyard—shooting hoops to help them work on their jump or foul shots—and shooting at my goalie in the yard as the day drifted off into the dark of night. Those are the times that I cherish—just as I still cherish that backyard time with my own dad.

The little boy arranged his blanket on the grass hill overlooking Lake Arthur. He fussed when his mom would reach over and try to put sunblock on—and he would adjust his small Sanyo boombox to the Pirates game or to Casey Kasem's American Top 40. He would get his tennis ball—and grab his brother and his dad and head down into the water and play catch. The smell of the standup top cooking hot dogs and fries would drift down and sooner or later he would wear out his dad and get the $2 for a small fry and a Coke. He didn't care about the hoop shorts he wore instead of a swimsuit—the big early 80's frames that were too big of course for his face and years later he would laugh at the old photos of—he didn't care that his socks were striped and pulled up to his knees as he walked back to the car at the end of another great summer Sunday spent with his family—his dad would always put the game on for the rest of the ride home—and you hoped the Pirates got a win that day.

We did a lot of family vacations when I was growing up—from the beaches of Lake Erie to Virginia—trips to most of the big cities that were within a day's drive (my mom is still afraid to fly) and yet it is those simple almost weekly one hour drives we would take to Moraine State Park as a family—just the four of us that stick out to me the most. We were blessed to be able to take our own boys to Disney and Universal numerous times…to Vero Beach two times a year for most of their young years—and to every big amusement park in the Northeast at least once. But it is the Sunday mornings we would wake up and just decided to load up the SUV and drive up to Moraine—good old Lake Arthur—that I realize were our true quiet time as a family.

Sunny (my beautiful cancer fighting better half) was not one to venture too far into the water so she would relax with a good book or the Sunday paper with her feet in the sand while the boys and I would grab a football and go into the water to play catch. They would use their water noodles or the paddleboards to goof on each other and with me. I can picture at this very moment—leaning on the rope that cordoned off the swimming area—waiting for my three rug-rats to finish tackling each other ten feet in front of me in the water and throw the ball back. I can picture looking up at the edge of the "beach" and seeing my beautiful wife and the throngs of people that lay on the hill…and of course—at the top—there was the smoke from grill at the stand still serving up those hot dogs—fries—and Cokes.

TIME—I guess as I have been thinking about what I could possibly share in this book that would make sense or maybe be in any small way be able to be accused of being insightful—I realize that besides being our most valuable asset—TIME can be a continuum—connecting generation to generation...passing the shared experiences of one father and his son—to the point that son has his own kids and he passes it on to them and hopes that someday they will be able to do the same.

At the end of the day it isn't a TV—or a car—or really any item that I received from my own dad—nor will it be any item or material thing that I will pass onto my boys that they will really cherish. At the end of it—it is the simplest of days—the uncomplicated pace of a slow spring morning or a summer afternoon that really connects us with our own—age to age to age.

But as I said the key is TIME. They can't share in your experiences if you don't make the time to share it with them. Instead of giving them stuff—the newest Smartphone—the newest gaming system…the newest pair of shoes—give yourself. That is what I have learned from this little experiment of writing this chapter—by going back to my own childhood—I realized just how much the dots really do connect from my dad to my own kids.

But recognizing is only a piece of the equation—if you don't or won't make the time to spend with your kids today—not only are you cheating yourself out of an opportunity you will never get to spend again—but you are potentially your kids kids—of the same experience.

So that takes me to my ultimate conclusion—the AHA moment of this exercise—who you choose to spend your time with today—and how much—doesn't just impact those that are around you now—those that you call son or daughter now. But your choice of the investing of your time—impacts the generation that will follow. Your grandkids—whether you are around to see them or not—may just be able to connect with you because of the shared experiences that transcend time—generation to generation.

Life really is not very long—even for those of us that may live to be a hundred—because one day—one day—one day our time will come to a close. That little hourglass with our name etched on it will empty out and it can't be flipped over. There is no more. Yet within the hourglass of time that each of us has on this journey we can control where we leave our sand—our mark—our footprint. But we can't make it unless we invest it—that sand can be sprinkled in a lot of directions over a lot of people—but as a dad I am thankful my own father chose to sprinkle his with me at a young age and I am blessed to have been able to do the same with my own boys.

That is all the wonderful insight I have; hope that it helps at least one more than it confuses.

Mark Carney Pittsburgh native and lifelong resident Mark Carney wears many hats as the widowed father of three sons—or as he refers to them in his social media posts—the man-childs. Austen is a now a freshman at Mark's alma mater Pitt. Logan is a senior at Plum High School and is off next year to pursue a degree in sports broadcasting and Nolan is a junior who besides a gift and love for the guitar is still trying to sort life out.

Sunny, the love of his life and the boys' mother—courageously battled a rare type of cancer for over a decade before finally getting her wings in November of 2012. It was during her battle where he learned how to put together and become a fundraising guru. The treatments for Sunny took them to Iowa, Tampa, Nashville, and most importantly three times to Basel, Switzerland. It was during her fight that he learned how to listen...what the true definition of a hero is...and what the real value of time is.

Now that his days as a coach for his boys' basketball, soccer, and baseball teams ended, he can devote time to growing his executive search firm which focuses on the Affordable Housing industry nationally. He also finally utilized his BA in Creative Writing from Pitt by continuing to keep Facebook busy—Sunny's blogs and is still patiently waiting to hear that one of the TV scripts/treatments he has sitting in LA is getting picked up.

He will tell you as he watches his man-childs grow that it is a blessed life.

Go Ask Your Dad

Chapter 2

What is the Most Powerful Road Sign?
By Nigel Brown

"He Who Knows The Why Masters The When" Dad

An octagononal STOP sign is the most powerful traffic sign on the road. It commands our attention and if ignored can have deadly affects. Our children deserve the same awareness and caution. At some point in our lives, every human being represented a stop sign. But, as fatherlessness continues to spread and dilute the family structure, fewer people are stopping to see the needs of our children. It's become normal for single mothers to coach their sons into manhood and sooner or later these mothers' stern advice becomes a faint whisper. The minute a son towers over his mother, the dynamics of their relationship change. Unconditional love will always be there, but without an active father to instill law and order, a young man's testosterone will begin to explore its boundaries. This is perfectly normal, but in a single parent environment most young men will look to other avenues to find balance.

Often, fatherless sons look for balance, approval and acceptance from the wrong places. Gangs are a breeding ground for fatherless children. On the surface, we see careless thugs, but beneath the foolish macho bravado associated with gangs, is a child who is screaming for his father. In poverty stricken areas many fatherless children don't leave the constraints of their neighborhood so personal growth is minimal. There are generations of fatherless sons who become fathers themselves and some don't know how to interact. Why? This is because the bar has been set extremely low. If a man never received anything from his father, he may assume that buying his son a pair of shoes is great parenting. By default, I fell victim to this mindset. My father was an addict so a relationship with him was never established. When I became a father, I gaged my interaction with my son based on my relationship with my father. My father and I never spent time together, so when my son's mother and I separated, I was more than willing to accept an every other weekend schedule. Now that I have a better understanding of fatherhood, I recognize all the time I lost with my son by agreeing to so little time. You can't build a sustainable, healthy relationship with your child every other weekend, but if you never received time as a child, you're blinded by this realization.

The world where I was raised in is much different from the world we are in today. Technology has advanced our culture on the surface, but we lack integrity. Technology has created a cyber playground, which has erased the parent/child relationship that once existed. Our children are creating online personas, which makes it more difficult for parents to understand their children. When I was young, there was a clearly distinct difference between my mother's generation and mine. My mother watched me of course, but she didn't care to be in my world. Technology has grouped us all together through our fancy gadgets; the days of sitting at a dinner table have vanished. Google replaced those awkward conversations about sex and our children are fending for themselves in a cyber Wild Wild West. It amazes me how unknowingly we as parents willingly gave our children over to everything the techno-world has to offer without guidance. You wouldn't allow your child to drive your car without knowing the rules and regulations of the road, right? And, even when they've been well instructed, you'll still worry. Shouldn't we have the same urgency when it comes to our children's Internet consumption? It's just as dangerous.

With the press of a button, our children become bait for pedophiles and murderers, but all we see is a phone. When I was young, there was such a thing as playtime. We couldn't wait to go outside and experience life. This newer generation has no concept of fun and many don't know how to interact with each other, which contributes to the level of violence we're witnessing. Video games have become extremely violent and play a dangerous game with our children's sub-conscience. The Hip-Hop culture isn't as colorful as it used to be with its array of messages. It has become a one-way street to a drug-infused abyss. Without a father to explain and model what integrity looks like, we're accepting the world's morals and throwing ours to the wayside. When will we as parents become a collective voice the industry will have to answer to? It's our responsibility to teach and protect our children, and I am convinced that any industry that has the power to transmit messages to millions of minds should be held at a higher standard.

Right? Without a collective voice for parenthood who is going to enforce our expectations?

When I was young, I saw how my mother struggled to raise two growing boys. She enrolled us into every sport known to man, and luckily we enjoyed it. This helped to disguise our need for a father at a young age. As we got older, things would change and my father's absence was more evident. Whenever I was at football practice and I saw a father supporting his son, I was in awe and I wondered what that love felt like. That feeling formed became a burning question, "How come I don't have this?" The question would become a seed that would grow into self-hate.

Over the years, I learned to suppress this feeling but I became rebellious in the process, which led me down a troubling path. Fast-forward thirty years; I stand as a proud husband and father of three children. My father's and my relationship never matured beyond my fourth year, but I forgave him and used his failures as my blueprint of what not to be.

One evening as I visited my father, somehow a conversation about football started, and I showed him a picture of me playing football in high school. He looked at me and with a straight face he said, "You played football?" The wound of being fatherless that I thought I conquered was opened like an old book and I was appalled. I immediately thought about every practice and game he missed since I was six years old. His comment gave me a new appreciation for my mother's unwavering love and support, and I realized fatherlessness has no age limit. I may be an adult and a better father than mine was to me, but my inner child still has that stop sign that he simply ignored.

Fatherlessness is difficult, but it takes a forgiving heart to start the healing. The bitterness associated with growing up in a single parent environment has destroyed our ability to salvage a broken relationship. We all deserve redemption and I made a choice to give my father a chance to reconnect with me.

Now, my relationship with my father is better than ever. We may have lost critical time, but every day is a new chance at forever. We have the power of choice and that gives us the ultimate advantage to stop fatherlessness!

Nigel Brown was born and raised in a single parent household in Baltimore, Maryland. As the oldest brother, and in a fatherless environment, Nigel had to take on additional responsibilities. Growing up in Baltimore wasn't easy. They struggled financially like most families in this concrete jungle. He vividly remembers the church taking up collections to keep them from facing eviction. Nigel's upbringing was difficult, but the love he and his brother received from their mother was always enough. During this time, Nigel developed a passion for writing. He used his mind to escape his reality and this outlet allowed him to find his true passion.

In 2013, Nigel Ali wrote a novel entitled, "Covered...The Fatherless Athlete" with NFL player Keion Carpenter. This novel walks its readers from childhood into adulthood and explains the effects of being fatherless through the mind of the athlete.

Nigel Ali is also the creator of the Stop Fatherlessness Inc., which is an organization whose purpose is to raise the expectations of fatherhood. As a husband and father of three children, Nigel Ali doesn't want another child to feel what he felt. Nigel has dedicated his life to make sure we all receive the blessings of a father's love.

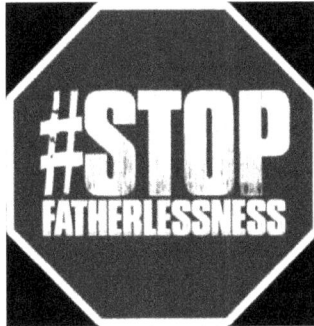

Go Ask Your Dad

Chapter 3

What Are Limitless Life Lessons?
By Brian P. Swift

It is easy being a father; have a child or several children. However the rewarding position of Fatherhood is not so easy and may even be quite daunting. Having a daughter or son and spending time with your kids, taking him to games, church, or the park and getting to know him or her is an example of fatherhood.

Fatherhood means being present (emotionally and physically) in his child's life. Make a significant difference in the developmental and behavioral issues of the child. This includes being an example weather that means washing the dishes, making dinner or taking the kids to school.

I am blessed to learn so many lessons and so much wisdom and I am not finished learning.

Know Yourself:

As a father I learned to deal with and overcome some of life's greatest challenges. We all face our greatest life challenges when we struggle with our faith, our family. We all struggle to find love, security and assurance that life truly has meaning. Our fears, self-destructive behaviors and excessive emotional struggles are caused by several things. One is our inability to interpret and correctly cope with our circumstances and feelings. Next is our lack of having a game plan. Also, we may not have surrounded ourselves with the kind of people who lift us up and push us to be better. As a child and young adult I was blessed to have a father and mother who always shared their wisdom and advice.

As a father of three adopted kids I preach the wisdom and advice I heard from my parents. As you get older and life becomes more complicated you must learn how to balance all the battles that you have spinning. We forget to balance all of the parts of our life that we continually need to balance in order to grow and move forward in life. Whether wrestling with chronic pain, mental anguish or a question of faith, it is possible to move beyond that place of hopelessness and get up and move ahead with our lives.

As unpleasant as it can be you must pause and consider your life. What areas of life hold your greatest challenges and what support do you give yourself? Is it your job/career; is it your relationship with God, your social life, hobbies or family? The fact is you must learn how to balance all of them.

Know that life takes care of the challenges and it is up to you to take care of the support. You must learn to seek support and wisdom from others, but also to appreciate and trust that support is available within, inside of yourself. You can draw from yourself the kind of support that will assist you best. For some it will be your parents you draw from. For others a coach, teacher, priest, boss or mentor may be the person who impacts your life the most.

You need to draw support not only to meet, but also surpass, the challenges. That is how you grow. Support plus challenges equals the best formula for growth. All of life is inviting you to grow, grow, and grow as you navigate the pitfalls of life. It is the resistance of supporting yourself through the challenges that create stress, tension, fear and unhappiness. Life is not about what you have. It's about what you do with what you have.

Know that life is not fair and that you will fail often, but if you take some risks, step up when the times are toughest, man up, put on your big boy pants and face down the bullies, lift up the downtrodden and never, ever give up, you will set the foundation for a successful journey through life.

Your Challenge:

I learned that my toughest opponent, the person that gives me doubts and the largest opposition to my success was the person staring at me in the mirror. Fatherhood will present this issue to you. The person in the mirror will be the person you have to conquer and find peace with in order to become the father you want to be.

I can tell you with 100% certainty I could not have successfully met the challenges that life threw at me without my trinity of Faith, Family and Friends. The relationship you create and nurture with your Faith, Family and Friends will be essential to your success. I have also been blessed with great mentors in the groups that I have surrounded myself; for example, my fellow coaches, family members and coworkers. I have also read many motivational books that have inspired me and taught me many valuable lessons. I use their words as guidelines to help myself and others. Find ideas, people and books that inspire you and make them a part of your life.

There are no secret shortcuts to a successful fatherhood. There are three letters that have kept many others and me on track. Remember C I A: Commitment, Integrity and Attitude. Look up the definitions and read how successful fathers and others define these three words. Then, approach every fatherhood challenge, every day, every situation and every obstacle with CIA in mind.

To the children & young adults:

Every generation gets tagged with a name, the baby boomers, generation X, the millennials, or the latest the "Y generation". If you are from the Y generation I have some advice; people are tired of hearing you cry and whine. 'Y' do I have to do that? 'Y' can't I make more money? Why can't I have that? Y, Y, Why, Why?

Stop asking why! Get off your computers, phones, and iPads and stop twittering, texting, and snap chatting. No one owes you anything and you are not entitled to things just because they exist. Your parents or the government do not owe you an education or a job. Not only do you need to stop asking why, you need to start asking how. How can I do that? How can I make more money? What can I do so that I can have that? You owe it to yourself to invest your own time, energy, and intelligence to discover how you can do these things for yourself. Stop blaming others and start behaving like a responsible person. Develop a strong backbone not a wishbone. Get out of the Y generation and into the now generation.

My Parental Responsibility:

As a father I believe that God desires for every father to step up and do whatever it takes to be involved in the lives of his children. More than just being there and providing for your children, a father needs to walk with them through their lives, and be a concrete representation of the character of God. Lead by example. If you can't handle this responsibility, don't have kids.

A father should love his children, protect them, discipline them, and teach them about God. He should model how to walk with commitment, integrity and attitude while treating others with respect. A father must teach his children to become responsible men and women who love their lives for what really matters for all time!

As a father, you are accountable to God for being put in the position of parent. You will blink your eyes only to wake up one day and realize that your laziness, job or your hobbies have no eternal value, but the hearts and souls of your children do. Regardless of the mistakes I made in the past, regardless of what my father did not do for me, I need to teach my children values, morals, integrity and to love. It is also my duty to mentor others who have no father in their lives, but who desperately need help and direction. The rewards are enormous.

Your Opportunity:

You have received a body and a mind that you may like or hate, but it is yours for as long as you live. How you take care of it or fail to take care of it can make an enormous difference in the quality of your life. You will learn lessons. You are enrolled in a full time school called life and often referred to as "the school of hard knocks." Each day you will be presented with opportunities to acquire wisdom and learn lessons; the lessons and wisdom presented are often completely different from those you think you need.

There are no mistakes, only lessons. Growth is a process of trial and error and experimentation. You can learn as much from failure as you can from success. Lessons and wisdom will be presented to you in various forms until you have learned them. When you have learned each of life's lessons, as wisdom evidenced by changes in your attitude and behavior, you move forward and can go on to the next lesson. Wisdom and learning lessons does not end. There is not a stage of life that does not contain some wisdom and lessons. As long as you live, there will be something more to learn. It is called "life-long learning".

You cannot love or hate something about another person unless it reflects something you love or hate about yourself. You have all the tools and resources you need. Remember that through faith, family, and friends you can have anything you want. Persistence and determination are the keys to success.

Many of us might like to devise a progress chart that we can refer to daily. Here's one containing the key ingredients for becoming and staying, a successful dad. It is a way for you to check to see if you are indeed learning and applying LIMITLESS LIFE LESSONS.

These Guarantees Include:

1. Choose Your Attitude.

Get your butt out of bed with a positive attitude and a game plan. Every day you can get better or you can get bitter.

2. Do Not Quit.

We all quit. It is necessary sometime. But usually if your brain says you are done, you are only 50 percent done. There is always more in your reserve tank.

3. Challenge Your Comfort Zone.

Many times it is only through discomfort and pain that you have the opportunity to grow.

4. Getting UP is the Key to Life.

In life if you don't learn to get up you will be walked on.

5. Patience is a Virtue:

It is an absolute necessity if you want to succeed. The secret is knowing that everything ends and your situation is just a moment in time.

6. There is a God and I am not Him:

7. Push Yourself, Seek the Harder Challenge:

Every week escalate your ability by pushing yourself both physically and mentally.

8. Priorities: Faith, Family, Health, Friends & Career:

9. Do Your Best and let God do the Rest.

10. The grass is NOT usually greener; you just need to start watering your own grass.

Brian P. Swift, is a Chicagoan whose neck was broken thirty-four years ago while playing football with his friends on the sunny, chilly day after Christmas, 1979, at the age of seventeen. As he found the courage and strength to recover, graduate from high school, earn his college degree, and earn his Juris Doctor degree as a quadriplegic, he also found his purpose: to achieve more than expected and to aspire to the best he can be.

After spending seventeen years in corporate sales and management he wrote his first book; Up Getting Up is the Key to Life. He shares his personal paradigm for mental, emotional, and spiritual recovery and facing the challenges of life as quadriplegic. It is the author's hope to inspire those with similar injuries and give hope to their medical caregivers, family, and loved ones.

The father of three adopted children and a husband of over 26 years, Brian developed his strategy of success, CIA: Commitment, Integrity, and Attitude. With his engaging style and practical wisdom, Brian will leave you invigorated to face your own struggles with hope, faith, and purpose!

After co-authoring his third book he started a non-profit called Swift Outdoor Accessible Recreation: SOAR. SOAR offers programs, services and equipment to improve the emotional and physical quality of life for people with disabilities, families, and individuals in need by creating outdoor accessible environments, soarnonprofit.com. Books are available at www.brianpswift.com

Go Ask Your Dad

Chapter 4

SENSEI SAYS?
By Bill Viola Jr.

"DO NOT PRAY FOR AN EASY LIFE, PRAY FOR THE STRENGTH TO ENDURE A DIFFICULT ONE."
                                        -BRUCE LEE

Simon says put you left arm up. Simon says touch your nose. Sit down. You're out! Having flashbacks to Kindergarten yet? Who hasn't played the age-old classic at one time or another? I often reminisce about those carefree days and wide-eyed wonderment of being the last man standing. If Simon was in your corner, it gave you limitless confidence; you could conquer the world. Simon could be your best friend.

The game, in its simplicity, parallels life. One person, the controller, essentially influences your next move. It could be a friend, foe, or even your subconscious, but someone or something is always telling you what to do. Either you listen carefully or stumble; make a conscious decision to follow the leader or deliberately disobey. Sometimes it's a sudden lapse in judgment—a mistake. None-the-less, at the end of the game, there are only a few winners. Life is tough.

At school, the teacher is the controller. At home, it's our parents. As we grow older the game is more complicated with bosses, spouses, friends, siblings, doctors, politicians, and of course your faith—God. You get the idea; it's a spider web of Simon's telling us what to do or not to do. To make matters worse, those

Simons begin to contradict themselves and pull you in opposite directions. Your wife says left while your mom says right. Your Pastor says up and your boss says down. Suddenly, you don't like Simon anymore.

While Simon is merely a fictional character in my game-of-life analogy, I grew up with a real life figure. In my household, Simon's reign was short-lived, replaced with a much more formidable figure—Sensei. You see, my father [Bill Sr.] is a pioneer of mixed martial arts in America and a living legend in the world of karate. The word Sensei (先生) is of Japanese origin, literally meaning "one born before." In layman terms, a Sensei is one who has experience—Wisdom. In my world, Sensei and dad were one in the same. The game had changed.

My father was born with strong Sicilian roots bearing the stereotypical fruit; a red hot Italian temper and equally famous short fuse. One could say nitroglycerine flowed through his veins. As Sensei, few dared to challenge his authority, but in rare cases the countdown began: T-minus 3-2-1 ignition! Fireworks! I laugh now, but Zambelli would have been jealous of the display. His fiery temperament runs deep, but passion may better describe his explosions. That "dynamite" personality allowed him to love as hard as he worked. He believed everyone had unrealized ability (aka potential). He saw something in me, and so our journey began.

The Viola family philosophy is steeped in martial arts tradition: discipline, respect and honor, so my home away from home was the dojo. One-on-one, each day we suited up for battle. He barked, "Pick it up; harder; how bad do you want it..." Those commands echoed wall-to-wall in a constant quest for perfection. Some days I was in the "zone," and others, sluggish. The tone and language could become quite colorful depending on my demeanor. One can imagine when Sensei Says, you sat up a little straighter. He employed a serious no-nonsense approach to working out. "Eye of the Tiger" became our adopted anthem and code for intensity! Only the strong survive, and we embodied toughness; mental and physical. I had to leave everything in the ring. Yes, Sensei could be a tyrant at times, but his mission was admirable. Why? To quote one of my favorite movies The Bronx Tale, because, "The saddest thing in life is wasted talent."

My father had a simple approach to training: "Monday, Tuesday, Wednesday, Thursday, Friday, Saturday, Sunday." So, day-in and day-out, my blood, sweat, and tears poured on the tatami (mat). When failure seemed imminent, Sensei would preach "will over skill" and somehow, someway, my mind prevailed. Under his watchful eye, I spent thousands of hours honing my craft. I was always the smallest, never the fastest, and certainly not the most naturally gifted athlete at the time, but was I gritty and driven. I possessed the intangibles: heart and hustle. He'd remind me, "Hustle beats talent when talent doesn't hustle." With his encouragement, I found a way to win, and I won over and over again.

There was no secret to my success; it was old fashioned, nose to the grindstone, work-work-work. Practice doesn't make perfect, perfect practice makes perfect. As Bruce Lee said, "Fear not the man who has practiced 10,000 kicks once, but I fear the man who has practiced one kick 10,000 times." Sensei was a stickler for basics and we laid the proper foundation. Each lesson was a challenge and each challenge a new milestone. My arms and legs would scream exhaustion, but the cries fell on deaf ears. Just before my breaking point, Sensei had an uncanny way to squeeze out one extra percent of effort. For that I am forever grateful. When I failed, it was haunting. When I survived, it was euphoria; an adrenaline shot of confidence you can't describe. In those moments, I had won a round of Sensei Says.

Victory was exhilarating, but being pushed to the limit can conjure love/hate emotions. While other kids played outside, I was hitting a heavy bag. While neighbor friends were glued to their

Nintendo, I was practicing kata. I didn't always appreciate the sacrifice, but I did obey Sensei. Deep down, he was strengthening me for life's battles.

For decades the same tattered wooden sign has immortalized Sensei's motto on the dojo wall, "The more you sweat in here the less you bleed out there." It's a constant reminder to train as if your life depends on it. I'm living proof of that dictum. Little did I know, slowly, I'd been assembling the building blocks of character: commitment, desire, dedication, discipline, and loyalty. Sensei Says became a domino effect. The work ethic and principals spread to my school work, studying for tests, or even helping a friend. I had become an over achiever, and no goal was unattainable. Sensei wasn't just preparing me for a fight in the ring; he was training me for the ultimate crown, the championship of life.

That competitive spirit has driven me to be the man I am today. I've never been satisfied with B's, second place, or vice president; I wanted the 4.0, the grand championship, the CEO, and have the executive parking space.

Obviously, I've come up short at different points in my life, but my confidence never waivers. It's a testament of Sensei's Molotov cocktail that always fired me up.

Even though Sensei ruled with an iron fist, he loved us dearly. I idolized him. His persona was larger than life, a man everyone seemed to respect. He had a certain swagger that people admired and gravitated toward. As a kid, I remember random men bowing to him at a bank or gas station. I didn't fully understand why, but I was enamored. Strangers would thank me for what my dad had done for them, how he inspired them, or pushed them to become successful. He wasn't just my dad; he was Sensei to the entire community. I wanted to be that guy.

I began to wonder, do I have what it takes? I began to think about my dad's remarkable focus and drive. Where did it stem from? I tried to imagine his childhood. My Grandfather and namesake (William Viola I) was a Don, the "Godfather of Brownsville," a charismatic figure who, for lack of better words, ran the show. He was loved by many, feared by some, but respected by everyone. Sadly, he cashed in his chips far too soon leaving my dad (an only child) as the man of the house while still in middle school. Those moments can break a man's psyche, but my father chose to fight. He fought for everything, every day to make his family proud.

His workaholic attitude was born out of survival; a determination fueled by the void in his household. He put himself through college and feverishly studied the martial arts. Soon he was teaching science by day while operating multiple karate schools at night. In between, he established a real estate and development company, and opened a sports memorabilia shop (at the height of the baseball card craze). As if that wasn't enough, he solidified himself as one of the most prominent fight promoters in the country. He was a master pitchman, negotiator, motivator, and teacher; the quintessential entrepreneur. I wanted to follow in my dad's footsteps. At some level, I was channeling my Grandfather's determination, courage, and moxie. In retrospect, my dad's success was paying homage to his father who never got the chance to see his potential. My father created his own way and vowed to protect me from the struggles he faced.

Sensei is a guardian. He wanted to give his children a better life, and sacrificed to give us that opportunity. His kids, all of whom earned their black belts, found success though his methods: two doctors, one lawyer and one teacher with a Master's in education. They entered the real world with no college debt, a gift from Sensei, and strong family support system. Each won a round of Sensei Says. I however, the first born, took the road less traveled.

"Sensei Says be a politician." Of course I followed orders and graduated Summa Cum Laude, naturally, with a bachelor's degree in Political Science. Gradually I began to second guess my decisions, but stayed on course. Sensei Says was starting to frustrate me. My passion was filling his shoes as a "Sensei," yet my aspirations, ignored. After college, "Sensei Says go to law school." For the first time in my life, I didn't listen. I stood still. My father's emotions echoed Vito Corleone, "I worked my whole life, I don't apologize, to take care of my family. And I refused to be a fool dancing on a string held by all of those big shots. I don't apologize, that's my life, but I thought that when it was your time, that you would be the one to hold the strings. Senator Corleone. Governor Corleone." It was if the script was written about our relationship. He quoted those lines to me in jest a hundred times, but a hundred times I refused.

I took a leap of faith and moved to Los Angeles to learn the entertainment biz. I wanted to be an innovator, a promoter just like Sensei, and thought Hollywood was the ticket. Sadly, I knew absolutely nothing about the industry. My friends and family were skeptical to say the least. I mimicked my dad's swagger, and walked in like I owned the place. I had instant success. Confidence is contagious, there is no other explanation. I worked with the biggest players in the business, everyone from Britney Spears to Arnold Schwarzenegger, and all along the way, despite my decision, no one was prouder of me than my father. I knew a conventional job wasn't for me. I inherited my dad's workaholic genes and proved everyone wrong. I was a dreamer just like Sensei and never looked back.

Flash forward seventeen years and I'm enjoying the last years of my thirties inching ever closer to the big "4-0." I've been blessed to wear many hats: son, husband, brother, friend, mentor, actor, author, teacher, film producer, fight promoter, fitness guru, trainer, instructor, coach; the list goes on and on. I've accumulated a treasure trove of experiences in my own right, but I still listen to what Sensei has to say. At 68 years old, my dad has seen the highest of highs, creating a new sport with all its fanfare, and the lowest of lows, seeing that billion dollar dream slip through his fingers. He's won, lost and finished everywhere in between. He's war-torn and softened a bit, but the glimmer remains. Over time, Sensei's commands have become less authoritative and more suggestive. The game evolved; Sensei was not just as a disciplinarian or instructor, but now an advisor, a mentor and my best friend. He's my consigliere. A day doesn't go by when I don't seek out his guidance, and likewise he consults with me. It's a new level of the game.

As the oldest child of five siblings, and the only boy, it seems as if I was preordained to be the next Sensei, although my father never wanted the stress or responsibility to fall on my shoulders. On August 17, 2010, my wife Jennifer gave birth to a precious 9lb 5oz baby girl, Gabriella Capri Viola. It was a game changer. It wasn't until I became a father myself that I fully understood the depth of Sensei Says. The cliché "someday you'll understand," had come to light, and his version of tough love clicked. Sensei was tough because he had to be, and the hard exterior complemented hard decisions; decisions that hold your child's future in the balance— Heavy. While I'm not quite as brash as my dad, some say more diplomatic in my approach, I've accepted my calling. The truth is, being a Sensei isn't for everyone, but everyone needs a Sensei. The ceremonial torch has been passed, and a family tradition continues. How we approach the game may be slightly different, but our end-game is the same—Confidence.

It's finally my turn to call the shots and want my little girl to chase her dreams; it's the only way she'll catch them. In the words of Paul Brandt, "Don't tell me the sky is the limit when there are footprints on the moon," and it's so true, limits are illusions. My daughter is the star of my universe. I'm her biggest fan and toughest critic; it's unconditional love. She's been by my side at the dojo before she could walk, beginning her own journey of self-discovery. As we navigate through life's turbulence together, I must steer her, teach her, inspire her, and motivate her. I pray each day for the wisdom to give her the right "instructions" in this crazy game. My father believed in me, and now I will do the same. Gabby's got passion, she's got what it takes, but it will take all she's got! I'm here to help her reach that potential, no matter what that might be. I know she'll make me proud; after all, she's a legacy.

Sensei Says, "The end."

Bill Viola Jr. is a Pittsburgh, Pennsylvania based producer, author and international martial arts champion who experienced the "Golden Era" of MMA firsthand as his father; Bill Sr. is credited as the co-creator of the sport (a decade before the UFC) by the Heinz History Center, in conjunction with the Smithsonian Institute.

Bill graduated Summa Cum Laude from the University of Pittsburgh in 1999 with a bachelor's degree in Political Science and immediately moved to Hollywood, California to gain hands-on experience in the entertainment industry. Subsequently, he earned acceptance into the Screen Actors Guild (SAG) and American Federation of Television and Radio (AFTRA) en route to establishing his own production company, Kumite Classic Entertainment in 1999.

He established Kumite Quarterly magazine in 2003, serving as publisher and overseeing distribution throughout North America until 2007. Viola is an accomplished freelance journalist, contracted by Sport Karate Magazine to cover the Sport Karate World Games on location in Mexico, Canada, and across the United States.

In 2014, Viola published the critically acclaimed non-fiction book, Godfathers of MMA, inspired by the life of his father. The book is the subject of the upcoming documentary film Tough Guys (2016). Viola has also served as an independent consultant for a number major motion pictures including the mixed martial arts movie Warrior (2011) and as an Associate Producer for the film, Tapped Out, (2014) starring former UFC champions Lyoto Machida and Anderson "Spider" Silva.

Bill teaches martial arts at the same school his father established in 1969 (Allegheny Shotokan). He is part of a growing Pittsburgh karate legacy that now includes his daughter, Gabriella Capri Viola. Although this chapter is dedicated to fatherhood, Bill notes that he was blessed with two loving parents. His mother (Shelley) was and still is a model of kindness and compassion.

Twitter: @kumiteclassic
Facebook: facebook.com/billviolajr
Website: www.godfathersofmma.com
https://en.wikipedia.org/wiki/Bill_Viola_Jr

Chapter 5

How Did I Come Out to My Kids?
My Journey to Truth and Happiness
By Chris Reber

My greatest regret in life is that when I was a young person I didn't have the courage to admit to myself – or anyone else for that matter – that I was gay.

In my defense, it was a different time in the 1960's and 1970's, with gay people widely closeted in fear and trepidation. The world was hostile and nearly universally uninformed about what it means and how it happens to be gay. Almost anyone who was gay in my childhood years lived in constant fear that others would discover this "terrible truth" about him or her. Although my parents were both loving and supportive of my brother and me in every way, I always doubted that they would have been accepting of my sexual orientation. They both passed before I was ready to share this with them so I will never know.

As a teenager and college student I convinced myself that I was bisexual and committed to and fully capable of leading a heterosexual lifestyle. While an undergraduate at Dickinson College I met one of the finest people that I have ever known and loved, and we were eventually married. During our twenty-three-year marriage Mary Kay and I enjoyed a more-than-comfortable lifestyle. We had very similar values and beliefs, enjoyed one another's company and doing things together. We eventually had two children – our son,

Jonathan, and our daughter, Katherine, whom we love unconditionally.

But as time marched on and the years passed, it became increasingly difficult, and eventually impossible, to be someone I wasn't. I knew that I was being unfair to Mary Kay and my kids by living a lie. The growing lack of intimacy in our marriage led to tension and brittleness that affected our kids and eventually every part of our life.

Eleanor Roosevelt once said, "You must do things that you think you cannot do." Although I didn't officially "come out" to Mary Kay until years later, we both knew what was wrong and Mary Kay and I eventually made the long-dreaded decision to separate and divorce.

Telling our kids, who were ten and eight at the time, was excruciating. We had to tell them we were divorcing, but they were too young to hear the core reason for this – that I was gay – and I wasn't yet able to acknowledge or articulate it at that time.

We met as a family. Mary Kay and I told Jonathan and Katherine that we both loved them and that we always would, and that while I would be moving away, I would always be their dad and involved in their lives. Having this painful conversation and leaving my family was the lowest moment in my life.

I lived and worked 90 minutes from the kids and for the next eight years they visited me on many weekends and holidays, and I attended school and other events in their home town. But I was not with them and I knew that I was not being the kind of father that I wanted to be and that the kids deserved.

Gradually society became more accepting of the LGBT community and I began to gain the courage to come out to those I loved, and, later, to others. It began with a few close friends and with Mary Kay. I knew that Mary Kay was aware but I had to have the conversation with her, and it was as difficult for me as it would have been years earlier when she hadn't known. Following my nervous and rehearsed comments, she calmly acknowledged to me that she knew this, and she was remarkably understanding and supportive. Had our roles been reversed I doubt that I would have been so understanding.

As the years passed, I increasingly agonized over when and how to tell Jonathan and Katherine that I was gay. How would they respond? Would they be embarrassed, ashamed? Would they stop seeing me? Stop loving me? It felt like I was carrying a million-pound weight on my shoulders.

Jon has encountered a number of challenging issues throughout his life, and I was doubly concerned about how he would react in view of these challenges. I didn't want to cause him emotional harm. Mary Kay and I consulted his therapist over a period of more than a year to gauge to the best of our abilities when the timing would be right to have this painful but necessary conversation.

Although I didn't plan the specific day on which I would tell the kids, a moment surfaced when I was with Jon, who was now 16, and the timing felt right. My heart beating harder than I can ever remember, and with a painful, sinking feeling in my stomach, I told him. I blurted it out using the most sensitive and caring words I could muster.

I will never forget Jon's response, which has forever changed my life. "Dad, it doesn't matter. I love you and I know how it feels when you are sometimes not understood by others." I later told Katherine and her response was very similar.

My kids' openness and love have made it possible for me to become a whole person for the first time in my life, and hopefully a better father and a better man. Their acceptance, support and unconditional love cleansed me of a lifetime of shame, guilt, doubt and fear. I feel like a new person with a new opportunity to live, love, support and help others.

After telling the kids, I came out to my colleagues and friends, who have been entirely affirming and accepting. While I don't choose to bring visibility to my sexual orientation, I also don't hide from it and strive to be a support and role model for others who may be struggling with sharing their story and their truth.

Angela Schwindt once wrote, "While we try to teach our children all about life, our children teach us what life is all about." My children have taught me a powerful lesson through their acceptance of who I am. Today Jonathan, Katherine and Mary Kay are also close to my husband and we are all an extended, non-traditional family. I cannot adequately express the depth of my feelings of thanksgiving and joy.

I am grateful for the opportunity to tell this story and thank my children and their mother for their understanding, acceptance and love. They are my heroes.

Dr. Christopher M. Reber, Chris, has devoted his entire 35-year career to higher education. He is currently President of the Community College of Beaver County (CCBC) near Pittsburgh, PA. Since arriving at CCBC in July 2014, Dr. Reber has led new initiatives in support of a student-focused learning environment, enrollment management, partnership opportunities, and a culture of planning, assessment and improvement, among others. He has led the development of nationally distinctive CCBC high school academies, articulation agreements with a wide range of four-year colleges and universities, and new programs to meet high priority workforce needs throughout southwestern Pennsylvania and beyond.

Prior to his current position, Dr. Reber served for12 years as Executive Dean of Venango College of Clarion University. Under his leadership, the college achieved record-breaking enrollments and developed a variety of new programs designed to address community and regional needs, supported by a growing network of partnerships with business, industrial, health care, human services and educational organizations.

Chris Reber's career also includes 18 years at Penn State Erie, The Behrend College, where he served on the senior management team in several positions including Behrend's equivalent of two vice presidencies: Chief Development, University Relations and Alumni Relations Officer during a successful $50 million capital campaign; and Chief Student Affairs Officer during a period of significant college growth.

Dr. Reber holds a bachelor's degree in Latin from Dickinson College, a master's degree in college student personnel administration from Bowling Green State University, and a Ph.D. in higher education from the University of Pittsburgh. He also holds a post-graduate certificate from Harvard University's Graduate School of Education.

Dr. Reber lives with his partner, Kerry Stetler, in Ellwood City, PA, and is the father of two children: Jonathan, age 19, and Katherine, age 17.

Go Ask Your Dad

Chapter 6

Can We Rise Above The Noise?
By Jesse Foster

As host of the Father Nation podcast I have interviewed a lot of Dads about fatherhood. Certain themes do come up quite often—such as the need to be fully present in the home, the need for patience, and the benefits of self-discipline. Another theme that relates to fatherhood in my mind has surfaced since I recently started working for New York Times bestselling author and international sales expert Grant Cardone. It is the idea of media influence.

Go to google news, or your Facebook feed, or turn on the TV, and you will see pictures of politicians, actors, sportsmen, and talking heads. Articles will confront you with vaccines, gay marriage, terrorism, shootings, and financial trouble with bubbles bursting ahead. There's a lot of noise out there. We are inundated with information from various angles with everyone having an agenda.

We live in a world with so many distractions. Now that we all carry our smart phones with us, the distractions—if you let them—never leave you alone. Many things are great about technology don't get me wrong, but you have to control it or it controls you. As a Dad, you have to set the standard when it comes to media consumption for your family.

There is a saying that you are what you eat, but the same could be said for what you choose to watch, read, and listen to. Take in enough of the main stream media and it will start to influence your thoughts. When you start having thoughts about something, it begins to develop into what I would call a "mindset", which is a way someone consistently thinks and sees the world around them. Your mindset influences how you act in life.

If you are drowning in the influences that everyone else is feeding on, how would you expect your mindset to be any different than the average mindset? Get an education, buy a house, don't talk to strangers, a penny saved is a penny earned. All of these thoughts and ideas are from the influences in our lives that eventually developed into our mindset on how we should act in the world and what we should pursue.

A mindset is like a worldview, a paradigm in how one sees the world. But the battle for your mind goes beyond mere politics and religion. You hold a collection of convictions on how this planet operates. There are many different paradigms out there, convictions that certain parts of the population have in regard to gay rights, multiculturalism, feminism—you name it and it's out there. A big one is what you can call "The Middle Class", a large portion of the population that operates under a specific mindset. Think of it like a pair of glasses. The right pair helps you see better, but if you put on someone else's prescription glasses, it distorts the world around you and prevents you from seeing things how they really are.

It's not good when such a large portion of the population watches the same media outlets, which are controlled by a small minority. If you choose to believe the media doesn't have agendas, then I'd politely disagree with you and challenge you to look more into it. The question is, do you want your kids feeding off of certain agendas, putting subtle ideas and messages in their heads day after day, month after month, year after year?

It's good to recognize the most influential ideas and values prevalent in our society and to understand the unrealistic, even irrational assumptions about reality from which they arise. Looking at it financially speaking, a clear understanding of your mindset is the first step in getting out of the middle class. Always remember that a mindset determines how you think. It is what allows you to deem something possible or to label something outside the realm of possibility. It's like a mental steering wheel that moves you where you think you should go.

Your mindset is deeply rooted within you. If you think about a tree, what you see along with all those around you are the leaves and branches which are supported by the trunk, but what supports the trunk? The roots underground, something you don't see, give life and stability to the tree. Your mindset is like the roots of a tree, and the only thing that the world can see is the exposed part, which is your actions. Thus, you can know a lot about a person—more than meets the eye—by his actions, or lack thereof.

If you are what you eat, and you are what you choose to watch, read, and listen to, does it not become imperative to be careful with not only the food you eat, but the media you consume? As Dads, many of us are careful not to let our kids watch what we deem to be inappropriate. Why then are so many of us not careful what we ourselves watch and consume? The media can influence us and bring about negative mindsets. Imagine waking up, reading about the latest shooting, a superbug traveling around Asia, a local motorcyclist getting killed in an accident, and a flood that has destroyed some homes. Does this start or end your day on a positive note? As Dads we need to be feeding on positive things; the world has enough negativity on its own apart from us voluntarily sucking in the news from the mainstream media agenda.

A positive mindset will provide a successful path in one's life. Attitude, albeit difficult to measure, influences so much. As a father and a leader to your kids, consider how the media has influenced you about the way you think about the world. Can reading and watching certain things weigh you down? I'm convinced that it can and does.

I'd challenge the Dads out there to choose carefully what media influences you consume. Your kids, even if they aren't seemingly directly watching—are watching. Don't assume that it makes no difference. I notice if I stop watching and reading certain things, after a week or two I start to feel less distracted by all the noise out there and can better concentrate on things that are important to me and my family.

When it comes to your money, if you aren't satisfied with the level of income you are bringing home, have you considered that the root cause of the problem goes back to your mindset? What has given you your mindset about what is "normal" and what you "should be doing"? Grant Cardone has said, "Average is a failing plan. Average doesn't work in any area of life. "In order to stop spinning your wheels financially, you have to give it more attention, more so than what society tells you. You grow up learning that you simply need to go to college; get a decent job and things will be fine. It's a lie. If you do what is normal, you will get what's normal—and that's financial struggles.

My message to Dads out there today is to rise above the noise. Don't be sheeple. Evaluate and think about media influences on your mind. Know that your kids will pick up on your seemingly small, insignificant habits that everyone else considers "normal". Just remember that to be anything extraordinary one must be different than the usual. This is how we can rise above the noise!

Jesse Foster is host of the podcast, Father Nation, where he interviews various dads on how to be a better dad. He resides in south Florida working for New York Times Best Selling Author and international sales expert Grant Cardone. Check out grantcardonetv.com for a positive media.

Chapter 7

Dad, What is The Master-Key?
By Lispert Dowdell

November 8, 1985, 12:01 AM. I cringed. My body went completely rigid as I watched a nurse draw a blood sample from the baby's tiny body. Thirty seconds later, I melted into a rocking chair embracing a twenty-one inch, eight pound four and a half ounce bundle of bliss named Lena Gail Dowdell. From that moment on I was hooked. When she looked up at me with those bright brown eyes, I fell in love for the second time in my life—my wife was the first time.

I was determined to be a diligent Dad. I became skilled in every aspect of childcare including: changing diapers, preparing bottles, cooking (which I learned growing up in a single parent home), washing and ironing her clothing, dressing her, reading the bedtime story. You name it. All while working full time. Of course my wife, who also worked full time, certainly carried her share of the load as well, and we had a pretty good support system. However, there was one thing I never quite mastered. Hair care! I was great at combing it and twisting it into a kind of ponytail, but I could never braid it as neatly and beautifully as my wife and my mother and my mother-in-law and my sisters-in-law did it. No matter how hard I tried, somehow the parts and sections looked crooked and disjointed. It haunts me to this day. So much for the myth of the perfect Dad, I am not yet him.

Despite the eventual revelation that I wasn't the perfect Dad, my daughter's birth reaffirmed for me the true significance of love. Love is the Master-Key. Love is everything. When I was younger, even when first married, I associated love almost exclusively with my feelings. But real love is much more than emotions. Feelings can change as quickly as the weather. Any number of things can, and will, change as time goes by and suddenly what was called love has faded or become something else. Of course, I'm not suggesting that love is, or should be, devoid of feelings but that it's something deeper and stronger. It's something beyond the realm of mere emotions. It's a place of knowing, deep in your spirit; a peaceful place, a place of ultimate commitment. A commitment that says no force on earth could ever change the love I have for you. A commitment that says I would gladly give my life for you if necessary. It's a commitment that comes out of a calm, deliberate, persistent decision that no condition or circumstance can ever change.

The funny thing is that I always thought I wanted a son. My two best friends and I would always debate about which of us would be the first to have a son. It turns out that two of us had a daughter and one of us had two daughters. Not a son among us. Nevertheless, I imagined me and my boy on the floor playing with his cars and trucks, flying toy airplanes and tossing a ball around. And yet, some of the fondest memories of my life are the times I spent at tea parties with my daughter and her dolls, or watching and waiting patiently as she prepared an imaginary meal for my consumption.

I remember how she beamed as I praised her culinary expertise, and I realized as she grew older how important praise and the power of words could be in the life of a child. Later, when she began to perform in school musicals and dance recitals, praise seemed to increase her confidence tremendously. She snagged leading roles in "Children of Eden", "Guys and Dolls", "Cinderella", and others. She even won a Mancini Award, which is the high school version of the Tony Award for students of Beaver County, Pennsylvania, (Henry Mancini's county of birth).

I learned a great deal about the power of words myself, and not just in the life of a child. I think my confidence soared as much as my daughter's as a result of her childhood. After all, there is nothing like the adoration of a child to boost the adult ego and even alter parental behavior. One thing I learned is that regardless of what you tell your children about how to behave they will ultimately do what they see you do rather than what you tell them to do. Yes, if you want a child to behave in a certain manner then, be an example. Model the behavior you want to see in your children.

When my daughter was a youngster, we were constant companions. Whenever I would leave the house she was always there asking, "Daddy, can I come?" It was very difficult for me to say no, and I rarely did. Unless it was a place that was inappropriate for her, I would usually take her with me. So, when I ran errands or dropped by a friend's house to shoot the breeze, or just went for a car ride she was there. She was very smart and amazingly inquisitive. She was reading at four years old, and I have never met anyone who asked as many questions in all my life. "Daddy, why does Mr. Smith smell like that?" "Where do cars come from?" "How does the telephone work?" "Where did I come from?" WHO? WHAT? WHERE? WHY?" HOW? Sometimes I thought I would lose my mind.

The truth is my mind grew sharper than ever. Whenever I wasn't sure of an answer--which was fairly often—I would say to my daughter, "I'm not sure sweetheart. Let's look it up." And so we did, and I learned a great deal in the process. I even began to ask myself even more who, what, where, why, how questions about many of the things I encountered from day to day. As my daughter grew, so did I.

So what is the point of my ramblings? Simply this: As daunting as it may seem, fatherhood is a wonderful thing; and it gets better with age. My daughter is now 30 years old, has a Masters Degree in Education, has lived in New York City (Harlem) for the past six years, teaches school in East Harlem and has a son of her own; a toddler named Langston (after the writer Langston Hughes). Each passing year from the time she was born until now has confirmed the wonder and beauty of fatherhood.

For instance, when my daughter was a junior at Kent State University she called home to inform her mother and me that she wouldn't be home for Spring Break, instead she would be going to Biloxi, Mississippi with other students to spend Spring Break helping victims of Hurricane Katrina. In these moments you know the satisfaction of being a parent, a father; secure in the knowledge of the things you taught and modeled to your child.

My daughter calls me regularly and lovingly admonishes me if I don't promptly return her missed calls. I relish the importance she places on talking with me on a regular basis and I realize it comes as a result of the time we spent together when she was young. You see, I discovered that from birth to about age 12 or 13 is a crucial period for Dad and child. Those tea parties, Q&A sessions, talks, car rides, and just goofing off, are more important than it might seem at the time. It's not some huge event or extravagant gift that your kid will cherish in the long run. What they will hang on to and build on are the times when you hung out at the playground on the swings or when you stopped by your favorite custard stand to get a cone.

When your kid gets around 12 or 13 they'll want to hang out with you a lot less than when they were younger, and that's all right (though you may not feel so at the time). They will probably have friends that they will prefer to hang out with instead of "old Dad," and this is normal. They may seem a little crazy at this age, but just continue to love them and be their father. Notice I said father, not friend. They will probably have more friends than they need. What they'll need most from you is to be a strong yet sympathetic parent. Children need a balance of firmness and understanding. Learn to be a good listener, and be straight and clear in the way you communicate. Though the average teenager hates to admit it, most understand that rules and boundaries are a necessary part of life. It's often how we, as parents, implement and enforce the rules that determine their effectiveness.

So let's sum up. These are my fatherly observations; and keep in mind that these are only my opinions, a few of the things I've learned along the journey of fatherhood:

(1) Spend as much quality time as you can with your children as they grow up. In fact, any positive interaction with your children is "quality" time. After all, time is the only thing that can't be replaced. So, spend some with your kids. They need you immensely. At about age 12 or 13 they will begin to need you more than ever, but they will think and act as though they need you less. As traumatic and frustrating as it may seem, hang in there. This too shall pass.

(2) Be the parent. Chances are your kids will have many friends. They'll need you to be their father. As they grow into adulthood the nature of your relationship with them will take on more of the characteristics of friend and mentor (but you'll always be Dad).

(3) Talk is (or can be) cheap. So model, in your words and deeds, the way you would have your children speak and act.

(4) Be straight and honest with your kids. Learn to listen well and you'll learn at least as much from your kids as they learn from you. Teach them to work hard, laugh often and not take themselves too seriously. Strive to be a man of integrity, even when no one is looking. And remember, your kids are probably looking even when you think they are not.

(5) Encourage and celebrate your children's uniqueness. Don't try to mold them into a carbon copy of you. You'll be surprised at how much they may resemble you in mind and body without any coaxing or instruction whatsoever. Genetics is powerful stuff. Nevertheless, they are not you.

Perhaps the most remarkable aspect of creation is that there has never been, nor will there ever be, anyone exactly like you. Even identical twins aren't precisely the same. So, help your kids discover their unique talents and gifts. Help them to be the best they can be. Encourage diligence and excellence. Don't compare them to others or tell them they're incapable, or allow them to fear failure. Lift them up, let them try, and try again. Let them grow; then let them go, and watch them soar!

(6) And finally, never forget that Love is the Master-Key to your relationship with your children (and all others). Everything you think, say, and do with regard to them should grow out of love.

"Love begins at home and it is not how much we do, but how much love we put into that action."

> "What can you do to promote world peace? Go home and
> love your family."
>
> *Mother Teresa*

Lispert Dowdell is currently the Assistant Coordinator of the Aliquippa Council of Men and Fathers/Fatherhood Initiative of Beaver County, an initiative of the Franklin Center of Beaver County Inc., in Aliquippa, PA., where he is a Father Engagement Specialist. Mr. Dowdell attended Northwestern University and the University of Pittsburgh, and served three years in the United States Navy.

Mr. Dowdell is a member of the Male Involvement Committee for Head Start of Beaver County and serves as Vice Chair of Head Start of Beaver County Policy Council. He has been married for over 30 years and has raised a daughter and helped in raising a host of nieces and nephews, and he is the proud grandfather of a two year old boy. In his spare time he enjoys playing the saxophone and flute, and reading. He is also a member of the Board of Deacons of the Triedstone Baptist Church in Aliquippa, Pennsylvania.

Dads' Exercise: Can You Pass A Fatherhood Quiz?

Are you Committed, Engaged, a Positive Influence?

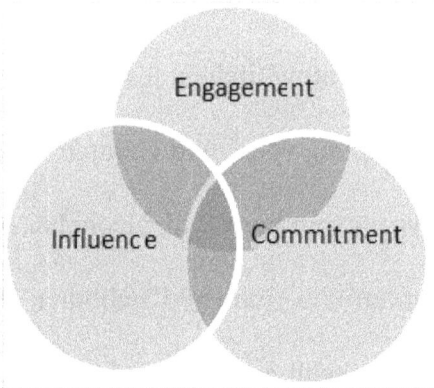

---

1. Who are your child's or children's best friend(s)?

2. What are their parents first and last names?

3. Who is your child's/children's bus driver?

4. Do you degrade authority figures in front of your children? Examples: parents, umpires, managers, police officers etc.

5. Are you remembering birthdays?

6. Do you find your eyes wandering to the screen of your phone while involved in activities with your children? Can you focus on them?

7. Are you participating in activities in front of your children in which you would not want them involved?

8. Are you kind to your pet?

9. Do you try activities your child/children like? Do you make them participate only in what you like?

10. Are you demonstrating lifelong learning?

11. Are you interrupting your child/children while they speak?

12. Are you abusing your body with alcohol or other substances?

13. Are you respectful to your child's/children's mother?

14. Do you have fun with you child/children?

15. Who is your child's/children's teacher?

16. What is your child's/children's favorite subject?

17. What are your child's/ children's favorite foods?

18. In what grade are your child/children?

19. What grudges are you holding?

20. Do you have a family photograph?

Chapter 8

What is a Dad's Battle?
By Dominick Domasky

Reasonably educated, from a home with a strong family structure, loving, employed, and committed is what my bio reads, as if I should be a perfect dad, and I was. My wife and I struggled for years to have our first child, so when the news of her pregnancy finally arrived I was ready. I cruised through her pregnancy and the first few years of fatherhood. My son was born and I was Super Dad. I was engaged, I loved, we played, I disciplined- it was easy for me. Three years later my daughter was born and although it was scary being the dad of a sweet little girl, I accepted the challenge.

Over the next few years, things changed, and I changed. My angel of a son was diagnosed with Type 1 Diabetes. My little boy now needed finger pokes to draw blood, shots to administer insulin, and a highly regimented diet. Every day mom and dad were the ones stripping his independence and he hated us for it. Rightfully so, we were the ones forcing him to poke his fingers before putting anything in his mouth and we were the ones sticking him with a needle anytime he did. I wasn't Super Dad anymore, I was overwhelmed, heartbroken, and feeling guilty for everything I did. My wife and I were clueless on how to help ease his pain, so we waited on him hand and foot. We were always there. Each of us made sure no party, school or sporting event was ever missed, so we could be there to count carbs and administer insulin. My wife and I were always there, out of love, but like a crutch.

Everything came second to caring for a child with Type 1 Diabetes; my daughter, my wife, and my job. I remember when we were staying in the hospital with my son after he was first diagnosed and telling my boss, "I am not sure if I am coming back to work." Type 1 always came *first* and that is what made it so tough when it was time for discipline. When my son acted out often it was a symptom of erratic sugar levels (a byproduct of Type1), but does that make his misbehavior acceptable? When he treated my wife and I poorly or his sister, was it his fault? Either way, there must be consequences.

Though confusing at times, I find strength and comfort admitting that I am not Super Dad. During those first years fatherhood had come so easily for me. My journey had been like that of a coach with a team of players more talented than the competition. My children were cute, happy, and healthy. Then adversity hit, and now I would be given the true test of a father. We fathers claim to love unconditionally, but what about when things are difficult? During this test I battled with my abilities and I battled with myself over how to properly discipline my children. My mind was torn contemplating whether I was being too strict or allowing my children to rule the roost. These battles were intense and when it came to disciplining my son, after years of struggles, I was at my wit's end. I tried deep breaths, checking sugar levels first, tough-love, softening-up, taking people's advice, implementing new theories and reading countless books on the subject, nothing was working.

My dad holds the most influence in my parenting style and he ruled with an Iron Fist. His mere presence commanded respect from my sister and me. My sister and I didn't talk back to my dad and we certainly didn't disrespect him. If he flinched- we ran. If he came home upset—we hid. Thirty years later, when I became a father and expected the same type of respect, it didn't work. My children didn't fear me, nor did they need to. Our society had evolved and in far too many homes, including mine, the children ran the show. Our schools taught our children about abuse, and at home and in the class our kids were spared the rod. Times had changed; there were no longer teachers disciplining with wooden paddles and if parents looked at their children wrong they were being second guessed. The next thing you know, we created a whole generation of children who were in command. These children held the power and if they told a teacher a story about their parents being too mean soon there was a knock on the door at home from a protective agency asking questions. The reverse happened at home, when a child said my teacher did this or said that; the parents were ready to explode. The children grabbed the power and parents and teachers lost theirs. Everyone took notice.

We live in a world of 24/7 over indulgence. As adults our eyes are seeing more things than even we can handle. School shootings, crime dramas, cyberbullying, ISIS decapitations, Police brutality and criminals shooting police officers; what's this world coming to? My son faces challenges and knows things at nine that I didn't know in high school. As parents we need more ammo, I can't take a knife to a gunfight and expect results. Our children are exposed to a constant stream of negative and provocative images and messages they're not equipped to handle. Turn on the television at any time or drive down any street and you'll see things that our youth's minds are not ready to process. There will be women in seductive clothing pushing products and ads for Viagra and beer. If you turn the channel or drive down a different street you may even witness wickeder images than the ones I described above.

Our children are like sponges and they're learning from every message and image they are exposed to. Dads, our children are seeing what we're doing even when we think they're not looking. Imagine their confusion when dad says one thing and does another. We teach our children to seek the police for help, but yet they see police violence. The line between right and wrong has never been greyer than it is today, and that's why it's our duty to be positive role models and not hypocrites. Dads, our children need our guidance because without a guiding hand our youth are unprepared to determine when they've crossed the line.

As for my ongoing battle, when I told my son to stop, he asked why? When I took a toy, he played with another. When I sent him to bed early, he raged. When I yelled, he yelled. Honestly, I felt I tried everything, but the situation was only getting worse. I spanked a butt. I tried time-outs. I took the bedroom door off the hinges. I asked for help, and my family even worked with a therapist. One therapist quit after five months, and three others came and went without making a dent. I was desperate, and my house was a ticking time-bomb. We all walked on egg shells because we knew each day there would be explosions, but we never knew what would set it off.

In a last ditch effort we tried jujitsu because we had heard the sport taught discipline. During orientation the school presented a checklist of parenting concerns that jujitsu could help address and I felt like I was given the magic ticket. We enrolled my son and during class he excelled. In class, the structure was having a great effect, but four months later our home life hadn't changed. The outbursts still happened regularly and my wife, daughter, parents, in-laws, babysitters, and I were all regular victims.

For my wife's birthday we went out to a special dinner and as a treat my son was allowed to order all-you-can-eat crab legs. Rather than being appreciative that his parents had shelled out thirty dollars for him to dine, he instead exploded because the crab legs weren't to his liking. A night of celebration was ruined by my 9 year-old's dissatisfaction of his crab legs. As I mentioned, my dad ruled with an Iron Fist. When I was young my sister and I weren't allowed to order a salad if it cost extra and here my son is yelling and causing a scene about the texture of his crab legs. This is definitely what they call first world problems, and my blood boiled, I'm not sure if it was my lack of a backbone or my son's sense of entitlement that made me feel worse. After a few threats and some uncomfortable moments at the table we made it through dinner without much more commotion, but on the inside I was fuming. They say never discipline in anger, however on this day I couldn't let it go. I had warned my son during his dinner outburst there would be consequences when we got home and I reminded him of this fact as we got closer to home.

My reminder started WWIII and no one in the family was safe from his venom. As we arrived home he yelled, and I yelled louder. I added punishments for every misstep and he got angrier by the second. After ordering him to his room and obtaining no results I moved him there physically. At this point, he swung, scratched, and kicked, and I squeezed tighter. In my mind I thought, what's next? My son continued his aggression towards me and I held him on the floor. What's next, I seriously didn't know because Dad was out of ammo. Was it time for me to call the police on him, did he need military school or medicine, or was I too strict or not strict enough?

A few days later, I was still disturbed by the incident and I reached out to my son's jujitsu professor for help. The professor was an ex-military man whose quiet presence commanded respect. He agreed to meet me after hours and I was hoping he had a magical cure. In my desperation, I thought maybe he had a scared straight program or a unique military experience that would immediately change my son's behavior. I started our conversation with a video from my iPhone of a similar incident as the one I just described. The intimidating but concerned professor immediately looked at me in disgust and quickly asked me to turn off the recording. Next, he looked me in the eye and said, "I don't know what happened before you started recording. And, there are two sides to every pillow. "

In the video my son had torn my shirt and he was yelling at his mother and me. I could be heard saying, "You don't put your hands on your parents and you won't be going to jujitsu this week. You'll sit out and tell the professor why you're not participating." In my mind this was fair and just, however, the Professor set me straight and in the process changed my life. The Professor said, "All that taking stuff away is bullshit parenting!" He then said, "I can tell you what your problem is," and he did. He said, "It's simple, your son doesn't respect you!"

Those words changed my life. He said what no one else had the guts to say, but deep down I knew. I am embarrassed to say, as a man from a good home and decent education- I was lost. I was blaming a disease, and aided by our softening society, but it was me who had created a monster. Unknowingly, I had spoiled my children and created a son and daughter who believed the world revolved around them. It wasn't a therapist's job or a jujitsu professor's to raise my children, it was mine. It's sad to say, but it took another man calling me out for me to realize my children are MY responsibility. It was my job as their father to take charge and no one else's. I needed to take accountability, and from that moment on I accepted responsibility.

That evening I asked my wife if I could take 100% control of our children's discipline. I asked for her support and assured her I would not hurt our children. My new policy was ZERO TOLERENCE and NO EXCUSES. Dad wasn't going to hurt the children, but I was going to kick ass. I decided I would no longer discipline in anger and my punishments would be swift and just. If my children were disrespectful, they would pay. If my children talked back, they would clean- if they had a problem with my punishment, they would clean more. If my children crossed boundaries, they would rake leaves. I would win, and I would kick ass. When my son got in trouble at school, soon after I made this decision, I called the baby-sitter to let her know I was coming to get him and things were changing. I carried my son out of her house and let him know things had gone too far.

When we arrived home, I didn't stop and check his sugar, instead I silenced my son and spoke in a stern voice. I said, "No more! Dad is in charge now. No more doctors, no more arguing, no more taking toys, no more early bedtime." All the toys and games I had taken, I gave back, but now I warned him there would be extreme consequences and no excuses. "Dad will kick ass! Meaning, get out of line and you will pay." I demand respect, and from now on I will get it. If we miss baseball because my children are pulling all the dandelions in the back yard, it's life; that's a choice my children made. On the other hand, if I let my children be disrespectful and rule the roost, that's my fault because it will be a choice I have made. They say, if you're fooled twice you're the fool, well times have changed and I won't play the fool.

Before my wakeup call and my decision to take responsibility my home was combustible. I made excuses. We had bad days and good moments. A year after my awakening we have an occasional bad moment, but mostly good days. My whole life changed by accepting a challenge and taking responsibility. My wife, daughter, and son are happier than ever before. If you're waiting for society to save you, you're in deep trouble. I no longer take a knife to a gunfight, instead I take accountability. Dad is in charge now, and dad is happier too. I owe it to my children to overcome adversity and help mold them into the best they can be. I now do what's best for my children whether they like it, understand it, or like me. Today we battle, but now we battle as a family, together as a team.

Dominick Domasky is the author of the inspirational book, *Don't Double Bread the Fish,* and creator and co-author of *The Unofficial Guide to Fatherhood.* His greatest accomplishments are his two children and he aspires to be the best husband and father he can be. He is a proud supporter of JDRF, an internet radio host, and a successful cold-calling, door-knocking salesman.

Mr. Domasky arrived at inspirational story writing and motivational speaking with a unique background. As a boy Dominick learned the value of hard work pulling weeds and doing odd jobs in the fields of his father's landscape company. He took those lessons of hard work and placed them into his passions, and carried it throughout every aspect of his life from basketball to business.

The Unofficial Guide to Fatherhood, was conceived by Dominick be a tool for fathers and caregivers to refer to in times of triumph or turbulence. Mr. Domasky admits the fact that he is not a perfect father; so, he enlisted the help of eight passionate fathers from across the country to share the lessons their parents and fatherhood have taught them. The dads who co-author this guide are all from different faiths, cultures, and upbringings and come together to create a guide that will help today's father succeed in an ever changing world. Today's fathers must be prepared to navigate the subjects of broken homes, teen pregnancy, social media updates, and drug addiction, but be strong enough to understand that true fatherhood is all about unconditional love and raising your children to be the best that they can be.

Don't Double Bread the Fish, Dominick's 1st inspirational book was not written from a pedestal, but from the trenches of digging ditches, picking up cigarette butts and overcoming countless failures. *Don't Double Bread the Fish* is not about Dominick, but thirty nine chapters of the modern day, easy to read lessons he learned along the way. Dominick will never pretend to be an Olympic gold medalist or business titan, and he'll be the first to admit he's just a guy who has failed, been benched, suffered setbacks, lawsuits, punches to the face, and got up and brushed himself off. Dominick has no ill will of the past, but looks back and finds humor and strength. As the old saying goes, "That which does not kill us only makes us stronger!"

Mr. Domasky is currently finishing his forth book *The Journey of a Grunt* which he expects to be published in late 2016 by Motivation Champs. Dominick can be contacted for events, speaking engagements, or publishing opportunities at www.motivationchamps.com or he can be found daily on Twitter @domd1000 sharing messages of inspiration.

Go Ask Your Dad

Chapter 9

Did I Get it Right?
By Dr. Fred Simkovsky

I have three sons. They are great but exasperating at times. What's new?

I was working the night shift and my three sons were just out of high school basically flipping burgers and bumming around.

One night, as I was getting ready for work, my three sons stagger in flopping over each other. We were in a 3 story town house and I'm at the top of the stairs as they roll in on the first landing,

My youngest one says, "Busted"! I look down and tell them to please come up to the dining room and sit down. They were really drunk! I told them I'll start making coffee so you can try to sober up.

The youngest says, "You are not going to yell at us?" I say no. What can I say to make you feel better or to try to stop you in the future? But I would suggest you three get it together before your mother comes home. That was more of a scare than me yelling. My father always said that when we got into trouble.

The next day I sat them all down at that table and told them that flipping burgers and getting drunk is no life. I asked, "Don't you want to do anything better with your lives than just what you are doing now?" No answers.

I said you have 2 choices to make now:

1- Go to college and I'll pay for it or
2- Go into the military; get a specialty like I did.

They opted for the Navy. I am an Army man but that was good.

Here's the getting it right for all of us involved:

- One of the twins made the Navy a 20 year career and retired. He has 4 kids and a wonderful wife. He is going back to college for a bachelor and master degrees. He is a certified ASL interpreter.
- The other twin got some more education and is a very successful maintenance manager at a large company. He has 4 sons and a wonderful wife. One is in college and one about to go to college.
- My third son is a certified database manager who wrote the Oracle test manual so others can become certified and now runs an IT department of a large company. He has 5 kids and a wonderful wife. One is about to go to college.

Results:

They all finally got it together and getting it right. My father, the cab driver and house painter was street smart with only a high school diploma. He knew to treat me and my brother as adults. I now hold several degrees as does my bother. My father was a great man and I didn't have the chance to tell him that long before he passed.

For me, I must have got it right because it worked! But it worked because I didn't yell, scream and stamp my feet. They were young adults and I treated then like adults. But I did put my foot down. **Tough Love works when it is done properly.**

It was a matter of mutual respect, love and caring. The bottom line is each have come back to me for advice and assistance with their kids. Each, over the years, has apologized for what they put me and their mother through. I told each of them that's part of life's learning. **That's Getting it Right!**

Dr. Fred (DocFred) Simkovsky is the founder and owner of LifeCareerBusinessCoach.com and Visions of Success Talk Radio Show, a 3 time, 5 star hit reaching over 4+ million weekly listeners in 142 countries, and an Emily award winning host, a certified master life and career coach with over 45 years of experience in multi-disciplinary environments both nationally and internationally in the USA, Canada, Germany, Japan, India, and China. DocFred has successfully guided over 1,000 individuals, at all levels, to their *Visions of Success* in the last 18 years alone. DocFred has 2 Amazon Kindle publications you will find interesting: Job Hunting and Recruiting, Everyone's Greatest Frustration! and Diary & Ravings of a Consultant from Brooklyn Or Being from Brooklyn helps, I think, Maybe, I don't know? FUGEDDABOUDIT!

His website is LifeCareerBusinessCoach.com . Use his scheduler to talk with him https://www.timetrade.com/book/WBZYQ or email him at mailto: fredsimkovsky@yahoo.com

Go Ask Your Dad

Chapter 10

Is There More?
By Jeff Jackson

There are a lot of demands on being a Daddy today, not just watching the little buggers themselves. Housework, cooking, dishes, laundry, putting laundry away, buying groceries and, of course, taking out the trash. I also ensure the house is stocked with all the necessary toiletries and cleaning products and bugger foods. None of those, except perhaps taking out the trash, have been traditionally "husband-ly" responsibilities. That's ok, I don't mind. It's a lot of work. But, wait, there's more.

I also monitor both of our cars and the house itself. Any problems with any of those, I usually take the lead to correct the problem. Whether it is the dehumidifier, the water heater, the furnace, the appliances, the oil change, the car inspections, etc. I deal with it! Plus, did I mention that the house also includes the yard? SMM (Sergeant Major Mommy has NEVER EVER done any yardwork!) But, I'm not complaining, just stating the facts. But, wait, there's more.

Besides all of the above, I also work full time. My job, as a full-commission salesperson, requires me to be on my game all day EVERY DAY! At least, every day I work, except on those occasions when my boss decides I need to correct something on my day OFF. I can work 50+ hours a week during the slow season and over 60 during a holiday or summer season, or holiday week. I work a lot, again I'm not complaining. I'm glad I have a job. But, wait, there's more.

Then, there's SMM. We need our time, too. Well, the bad news is that even though she doesn't put in as many hours as I do, her commute is 45-60 minutes ONE WAY every day over the Tappan Zee Bridge, which is collectively and universally known as the world's largest parking bridge. The good news is that we know we have some special little buggers. We support each other unconditionally and lovingly, unless she wants to watch one of her "shows" in which case we at least take turns in case I need to watch an "important game." Since she spends more time with the little buggers, she cooks more than I do, helps with homework more, cares for her mother who lives with us and cleans the house more. She is also usually responsible for taking the buggers out to birthday parties or shopping or errand running.

SMM and I try to split our responsibilities 50-50 with the kids and the house. In reality, she probably does more than I do, so it's probably closer to 60-40. As much as I proclaim I do, mommy does even MORE. But, wait, there's more.

The little buggers need their mommy and daddy time, too, don't they? Well, of course. We don't play favorites and we switch and go back and forth to help and spend time with each one individually. Unless, of course, one of them decides to play Cheetah Tag or Ghost Plane or House Excavator and they require IMMEDIATE assistance and guidance so as not to hurt themselves or each other or the house or our constitutional freedoms. Not to mention, the buggers have an insane amount of homework every night. Plus, they have started Tae Kwon Do classes, which they have been doing for about four months. But, wait, there's more.

You can see these activities take a lot of time, energy and attention (and the elusive and fickle dollar). The twenty minutes or so I have left every day to "veg out" or "wind down" or "medicate" my intense stress and traumas during the day, I spend on the computer searching for the Meaning of Life on social media or, at least, a laugh. Or both, if I'm lucky.

Of course, there are a few things I wish I had more time to do. I would like to spend more time on my writing and would love to do this professionally. My mission is to entertain and lighten the load of Daddys everywhere by sharing MY "story." Individually, I believe Daddys are appreciated. Collectively, culturally and socially, may be not so much.

I wish I was exercising more. In my youth, I played all the sports and was pretty good in them. Baseball and swimming were probably the two sports I was best at. And as much as I loved to play basketball, I was always a scrawny kid who could shoot well, but didn't have enough strength and muscle to compete on a higher level.

As I've gotten older. I've moved away from team sports and have worked out individually. I don't have the resources (as mentioned above) to participate in team sports. My wonderful wheels served me well in my youth, but are not as strong or as flexible in my old age. Hey, I'm middle-aged. Can't deny it. Can only sugar-coat it so much.

The biggest thing I never really anticipated was that EVERY TIME I SIT DOWN WHILE I'M WATCHING the little buggers, I have to get right back up again. EVERY TIME! Unfortunately, that doesn't really count as aerobic exercise. And my job which requires that I stand 10 hours a day doesn't really count either. And my finger workout on my keyboard has no merit as exercise.

I suppose it was easier for my dad. I think about him almost every day. Society was different, much simpler, back then. I think of Mommy, too. They didn't have all the stressors we have today. No computers, no cable TV, no cell phones. Dad worked every day and mom stayed home. I envy them for that.

They've been gone for some time now. I wish I could talk to him and get advice or support or comfort. Even though he never talked very much, he was always there when I needed him most.

Dad had five kids. I have two. He worked full time at a job he hated. But, just being a high school dropout, his choices were limited. He eventually got his diploma going to night school. I remember missing the Mickey Mouse club because we would have to go and hang out at school while he was in class. It was only one night of the week. The bad news is that he got only a little bit of recognition and promotion for it, but it never panned out the way he wanted.

When I went through a tough time in my early adulthood, it was my Dad who got me on the right track again. He found me a job and chauffeured me to work every day.

I eventually got focused again and went back to college and even on to a Master's degree. I got married and moved. Then, the world again turned upside down and I got divorced and changed jobs, then careers.

My Dad was originally from New York City, so that's where I went. I had always wanted to live there. I said it was to pursue my professional acting career, and it was, but I think there was a deeper meaning than that. I think I wanted to find out more about my Dad's origin and upbringing.

New York is the greatest city in the world, but it is definitely not for the faint-hearted. Not that I was involved in any violent or aggressive activities, but I had to share my world with 8 million of my closest friends. Plus, my Dad still had family and friends there whom I came to know and love. And I came to understand my Dad better by listening to them talk about his early life.

Eventually, I met my wife; we moved out of the city and had two glorious sons. My professional acting career lasted only a couple of years, but it was worth it. I had my chance to live in Manhattan for two and a half years.

I like to think I'm older and wiser now, but in reality, I have my good days and bad days. Even though I am in a job which, quite frankly, doesn't use my education, it suits me well and has provided for me so that I can provide for my family. I didn't drink for the boys first seven years of life and now, only have a glass of wine occasionally before bed.

I remember my Dad stopping the car, in pouring rain, because a woman's car was stopped at an intersection. We offered her a ride and drove her to the nearest gas station. My goal is to be the role model for my boys that my Dad was for me.

In the overwhelming midst of taking care of myself and my family, I don't want to neglect the rest of the world. I want to enjoy the little buggers' childhood, too.

There is a lot on my plate to be a Daddy. It is a lot of work, which seems to grow every day. The good news is that I enjoy it and am meeting the challenges head on thanks to experience and training and a supportive wife and mummy. The bad news is that someday the little buggers will be all grown up and have their own lives. That's life. I don't know if there is anything more than that.

Jeff Jackson was born and raised in Dayton, OH where he attended Wright State University and earned his undergraduate and graduate degrees in business. After working in corporate America for a number of years and a divorce, he moved to NYC to pursue his lifelong passion for acting. However, life had different plans.

Jeff became a daddy "later in life" and is now married to a wonderful wife and mommy to their twin boys. For the record, he did not have any gray hair before they were born!

He is a husband, daddy, writer, salesman and superhero in training and lives about 30 miles north of NYC. Jeff actively supports men and daddies to be their best.

Check out his blog www.DaddyisBest.com to get a glimpse of the trials and tribulations of raising twin sons. Hopefully, you'll get a chuckle out of it, too.

Dads' Exercise: What are Some Famous Dads Saying?

What would you want your quote to be?

"Do I want to be a hero to my son? No. I would like to be a very real human being. That's hard enough."

Robert Downey Jr.

"Above all, children need our <u>unconditional love</u>, whether they succeed or make mistakes; when life is easy and when life is tough."

President Obama

"Fatherhood is the best thing that could happen to me, and I'm just glad I can share my voice."

Dwyane Wade

"It is a wise father that knows his own child."

William Shakespeare

"My father gave me the greatest gift anyone could give another person – he believed in me."

Jim Valvano

"I made a decision when my father passed away that I was going to be who God made me to be and not try to preach like my father."

Joel Osteen

"When I was a boy of 14, my father was so ignorant I could hardly stand to have the old man around. But when I got to be 21, I was astonished at how much the old man had learned in seven years."

Mark Twain

"I became a father for the first time, at age 43; my greatest achievement! It was followed by a second and a third, at 3-yearly intervals. Each birth made me---unashamedly---prouder, for them, for making it into this world and becoming such worthy human beings."

Joe A A Silmon-Monerri

I have found the best way to give advice to your children is to find out what they want and then advise them to do it.

Harry Truman

"When you feel that being a Father is just too hard, remember to laugh and silence the world and say, 'We should go up and take possession of this thing called Fatherhood, for we can certainly do it." From What God told me the night before I became a father."

Eduardo Quintana

Steve Harvey once asked Bob Paff, "What are the three things most dear to you? "My family, my faith, and my failures; I think the greatest lessons in life come from our failures."

Bob Paff

WHAT IS YOUR QUOTE? _____

_____

Go Ask Your Dad

Chapter 11

Can I Become the Dad I Was Meant to Be?
By Howard Upton

I liken finding out about becoming a father to that of someone moving through the five gates of grief, and in many cases I believe men do, at first, grieve the news. Most men will move through the psychological stages after being told about their impending fatherhood:

- Denial (This can't be happening to me—I'm not ready)
- Anger (I'm never going to be able to watch another game in peace!)
- Bargaining (Please God, won't you still allow me to hang out with my buddies on Friday nights and on game day?)
- Depression (My life will never be the same. Life is over!)
- Acceptance (I'm okay. I will teach my kid how to enjoy the game, or at least be quiet while I'm watching.)

Without exception for any man, fatherhood is the single-most life-altering event imaginable. When the doctor first places that little bundle in your arms, you are inevitably forced to consider your future; although as most would agree, we are a little selfish in our introspection. Having a child changes everything, and I do mean everything.

Even though we may "try" to have a child, it is oftentimes difficult for a man to wrap his head around the reality that his wife is pregnant and will soon give to him another living, breathing human being dependent upon its Mom and Dad for EVERYTHING!

I know what you're thinking—being a Dad should never be compared to grieving. Look, in no way, shape, form, or fashion am I saying that fatherhood is an event to grieve; on the contrary, becoming a Dad was the most important thing that has ever happened to me, and I suspect it was, or will be, for you too. The bottom line is that men, no matter how much we attempt to prepare ourselves to have a little person invading our space (a baby that is exactly one-half us, and a child that will forever be interconnected to us), our minds struggle to grasp that reality.

Once we accept that our lives will be forever changed, and that someone will depend on us for the remainder of our days—once we are no longer overwhelmed by these thoughts, we can move on to becoming the Dads we were meant to be. Wow! "The Dads we were meant to be." That is a pretty strong statement, isn't it?

I was in the delivery room for the birth of both of my daughters, and each time I was mesmerized with the miracle of life. Much more than being amazed at their arrival into the world, I was overcome with a primal sense of being their protector. After all, this was my flesh and blood I was holding in my hands.

My mind was filled with thoughts of what I wanted to teach and show my girls. There was an enormous world out there and I wanted to make sure they experienced all of it in a healthy, education-filled, and loving environment. Yes, I envisioned winning the prestigious and mythical "Father of the Year" award and displaying it proudly on my mantel. Unfortunately, I was a young Dad with no knowledge of rearing a child, other than having been raised by a southern, military laden father who raised two boys. Oh, and I did not own a mantel either.

My oldest girl was walking at seven months and speaking in complete, albeit short, sentences at nine months. You cannot imagine the sense of pride she instilled in me, as visions of Nobel Prizes being awarded to my genius child filled my brain. She caught on to everything so quickly and was perfectly beautiful—yes, the fruit of my loins was destined for greatness!

On the opposite end of the spectrum was my youngest daughter. She refused to walk or talk. Her vocabulary at two years of age was limited to a handful of words. Expressing little interest in standing up, much less putting one foot in front of the other in order to be mobile, my youngest was content to sit around and grunt and watch those who would fend for her. I told her mother I feared some form of mild retardation had inflicted our daughter.

Courtney, our oldest, began school and excelled. Her teachers raved at her penchant for learning and insatiable thirst for knowledge. Cassidy, the baby, continued to point and grunt for things she wanted, and because my diagnosis of some mental ailment was probably true, we obliged. It appeared we were in for a life-long endeavor of caretaking.

When Cassidy turned three, we elected to put her in daycare. Suddenly, she was capable of talking and walking! We were simultaneously shocked and relieved at her miraculous recovery and thankful for those at the daycare center who obviously aided in her cognitive rehabilitation.

Over the years both girls grew smarter (and walked normally) and excelled in their school work. Each girl had a decidedly different personality and disposition; Courtney was extroverted and a tomboy, Cassidy introverted, shy, and girlish. Oftentimes, I wondered if the two were truly related and marveled at the fact that they shared the same genes.

The dreaded day came when the girls brought boys home as they began dating. It was unfair to me, the man who had given them life, helped nurture and comforted them when they were sick, changed nasty diapers, and took them fishing. How could they forsake their father for some young, acne bearing punk they barely knew?

The deck of cards life deals is rife with jokers. I was my daughters' protector, the purveyor of truth and justice in their young lives. My lack of knowledge in raising two girls had come full circle, as I watched both grow into beautiful young ladies. Courtney is now engaged, finishing her undergraduate degree and living apart from her Daddy. Cassidy is a senior in high school and preparing to enter college very soon.

As I look back on the last several years, I struggle to remember what it was like prior to their births. At the beginning of this chapter, I explained that men about to become fathers sometimes struggle with the actualization that they are about to lose their singularity and enter a world of plurality. The honest truth is my memory of life before my children is blurry, but life *with* them is clear and full of happy thoughts and recollections.

On several occasions I have thought about what I have shared with my daughters—sometimes tough- love, life-lessons, discipline, a desire to better ourselves, a love for the written word. However, in my heart-of-hearts, I know that what I have shown and taught them pales in comparison to what they have taught and given me over the years.

Before my children were born, I was impatient, hot-headed, self-absorbed, and career-driven. What mattered most to me was a progression of self, without room or tolerance for those who would get in my way. My girls changed all that (well, I am still career driven, but I have managed to temper that over the years), and forged in me something I did not know existed: a man capable of loving beyond measure, while still holding firm to his moral beliefs.

Children will, and have in me, make you the Dad you were meant to be. They will make you laugh, cuss, cry, and jump for joy. Kids will make you, Dad, prouder than any personal accolade or award you may have won, and they will break your heart over the course of your life. All of these events will change you, even though you may not realize it at the time.

Enjoy every moment of your children. Do not be afraid to play dolls with your daughters or go outside and throw the ball with your boys. These are the memories that will resonate with you, be most clear in your mind as you age, and last over more than just your lifetime.

Howard Upton is an accomplished action/adventure fiction novelist, whose past includes playing college football, winning a national championship in powerlifting, earning a Ph.D., traveling the world, and most importantly, being a Dad. He and his wife Cathy reside in his home state of Alabama where he cheers on the Crimson Tide and loves the mild winters. Howard has authored two books, *Of Blood and Stone* and *Occam's Razor*, both of which are available through Amazon and his personal website.

Howard can be followed via social media at:
www.facebook.com/howardsauthorpage or contacted through his website:
www.howardupton.com

Go Ask Your Dad

Chapter 12
How Do I Make a Positive Impact?
By Reece Anderson

It was another routine supermarket run. I just had to make a quick call to my wife for some clarification on what was needed for our evening meal. She answered after one ring with a "Hey!" There was something unusual in her tone as we talked through the mundane ingredients needed for dinner. As I turned the corner to walk up the next aisle I had to step aside to allow a heavily pregnant lady pushing a trolley past; it was at that moment, Vicky said the words "Reece, guess what? You're going to be a Dad".

Like most men hearing these words from the woman they love more than anything in the world I was ecstatic. But as this pregnant stranger passed and we briefly made eye contact I got this lingering feeling in the pit of my stomach.

Then the thoughts and fear started to hit me... "I am not ready for this", "How can I be a role model for someone else when I still feel so lost in my own life?" How was I going to share love when presently I was struggling to love myself'?

Fifteen Years prior I had been sitting at home when I was hit with an unbearable surge of anxiety. It felt like I was in a sprint race but I was standing completely still. My heart had elevated to 160 beats per minute. I was 20 years old when I suffered my first panic attack. Young, naïve and in desperate need for a 'cure' I diligently started taking a daily pill prescribed by our family doctor, which quickly turned into 2, 3 and then 4. That was the beginning of a long journey of pain, self-doubt and continual numbness.

The day I discovered I was going to be a father, I had been off my medications for four months. Years of popping multiple tablets on a daily basis had left devastating effects on my mind and body and right at that moment I was wishing I still had them.

A different kind of anxiety was hitting me in that moment; in just eight months I was going to be a father, a husband and a provider. The weight of it all seemed too much. How was I going to be all of that when I was struggling just being me?

I wanted to rise up to the challenge and conquer the doubts running through my head; but firstly and most importantly I needed to begin loving myself. I needed to start embracing my imperfections, acknowledging my strengths and looking at my reflection in the mirror and saying, "Reece, I love who you are as a person".

With a child on the way this idea of love consumed me. I was constantly contemplating how people give love and receive it, what did it look like? How did it feel? Mostly though, I thought about how love looked through a child's eyes.

As a child, I viewed my father as a hardworking man who would do anything for his family. My parents were resilient and they taught us to be the same. My father showed love through his actions, he was at every soccer game, running competition and tennis match. He worked over-time to ensure that every year we had our annual camping trip to a neighboring seaside town. This was my father's way of showing us love.

I had a good childhood, I'm grateful that I can look back on many fond memories of laughter and togetherness. While on this journey of self-discovery I realized that I held much the same values as my parents, with family at the epicenter of everything. But as I was unraveling my own story it became apparent something had been missing, It was something that I could see I was not doing a lot of and my wife had made mention of more than once... and that is showing love through affection.

Love is a very broad word that is used flippantly and thrown around like a boomerang these days. But for me it's quite simple, 'love is that condition in which the happiness of another person is essential to your own'.

Love can be expressed in many ways, but the opportunity is often missed. As a man on a mission to understand himself more I looked back at my own childhood and realized what had been missing from the people who taught me how to love, my parents. Whilst I felt my parents love on a daily basis I find it hard to recall a time during my childhood where I witnessed my parents affection for one another; whether it was a kiss, hug or simply reciprocating respect. The thought of becoming a Dad really got me thinking that this is something I wanted my wife and children to feel and see.

As a man there have been times when speaking words of affection have caused me to tighten up, even cringe a little; as if somehow these words may lessen my masculinity. Displaying affection was something I hadn't been taught by my parents. In fact, the only time I ever witnessed any form of affection between my parents was when I was in my late twenties. I remember surprising myself with the emotional reaction I had to it. This ruse of affection came after my parents reunited after a trial separation. I could see that it was not authentic and it would not last. In that that moment I was angry because I knew my Mum wanted affection all the time, but my Dad through no fault of his own just did not have the tools or the upbringing to give that to her. My Dad had been brought up to be a provider for his family first and foremost.

There were many times my Dad could have given me a hug. At the peak of my anxiety when I was unable to work, he seemed the furthest away. We have since spoken about this period in my life and he admits he just didn't know what to do or how he could help me.

As a father and a husband I want to ensure the environment I create at home is full of love and affection. I believe when children see a father and mother openly express love and affection it creates stability, sense of belonging for the child. What was worse than seeing my parents argue, was that there was never reconciliation. As a child, I would shake with fear when I my parents fought. I had taken those memories and behaviors subconsciously into adulthood; for a long time I thought raising your voice and waving your arms when in disagreement with loved ones was acceptable.

Without realizing it I had become the type of man I didn't want to be; the one who didn't display affection, didn't treat or talk to my beautiful wife in a loving and compassionate manner.

The effects our relationship could also be seen on my stepdaughter. When Vicky and I fought she would begin retreating into a shell, just like I used to when my parents fought with each other. Looking back I have always had a habit of acting on pure emotion and using this to justify talking down to people. For a long time I had little awareness of what damage this could be doing to our relationship and the people around us.

We often look at the external influences affecting our children and pay less attention to what's going on at home. We want the best for our children, but rarely stop to consider the values we are instilling upon them through our own actions. If our children are witness to parents who disrespect each other, are quick to anger and show no affection they will grow into adults thinking that this is the norm. I know I want more for my children.

Being a father is a privilege, it is our chance to nurture, set an example, instill values and provide children with a stable environment and a sense of belonging. As parents, if we display a loving affectionate relationship toward each other, we are setting the benchmark for the future relationships our children will have. They will expect nothing less than love, affection and mutual respect; it will always be in their heart and their head to expect nothing less. As a man for whom displaying affection does not come naturally it can be easy to become complacent, but I want more for my children.

I have a chance to cease this cycle of destructive behavior, to become a better man, father and husband.

I am now a proud father to my 4-month-old daughter Eden Rose, step father to 9-year-old Belle and have a great wife in Vicky. I am challenged every day to become the loving, affectionate man I strive to be. Through my fifteen years of being medicated my emotions were so suppressed that all I knew was anger and frustration. I was heading in a direction where showing love to me was unthinkable let alone showing those closest to me.

From the day I came off that last pill to when I found out I was going to be a father I worked on me. I not only worked on the man I wanted to be for me, but the man I want to be for my family. It is true what they say; you can't pour from an empty cup!

I just wanted to be able to show love and affection to my children and my wife and it helped by loving me first. I look in the mirror now and love the man looking back at me and because of this, love now flows through our household. Every day I am growing. Every day I am making a conscious decision to being affectionate to those closest to me. I want my children to grow up seeing Mum and Dad respecting each other, displaying affection and giving them the best role models possible.

It has been a challenging ride having to open myself up to the possibilities of what I wanted to become. But if it came easy I would not have discovered me, I would not have discovered how much affection and love were missing in my life and the effect it was having on those around me. My kids now have a father who has become more open and loving. My personal journey has made me face many obstacles, but nothing is more satisfying than finding the affectionate father in me.

Reece Anderson is a married father of two who was born in Wellington New Zealand; he currently resides in Brisbane, Australia where he has lived for the past 10 years. Reece has worked in Management for most of his adult life, but his real passion is in coaching and mentoring others while sharing his experiences in overcoming debilitating anxiety, depression and tics (involuntary body movements).

After growing tired of the side effects brought on by taking various prescription medications, Reece made a decision to stop taking the drugs he had been prescribed for 15 years and seek alternative treatment. This was the beginning of a long and difficult journal of self-discovery, emotional, mental and physical healing.

Reece is now 18 months without any medication and is in the best mental and physical shape of his life. Reece hopes to share his experiences with others and is an advocate for alternatives treatments for anxiety and depression.

Chapter 13

What Was It Like Growing Up in Aliquippa?
By Shon Owens

Growing up in Aliquippa PA, was at times an awesome experience as a child, playing football on the playground with the guys, going to school, trading baseball cards, playing marbles, and a host of other childhood memories I hold dear to my heart, but there was still something missing in my life and I could not put my finger on it. When you're a kid you can't quite articulate the emptiness that you feel, but you definitely know that there's a void in your life. Despite all of the fun I had as a child the one thing I wanted most was my Dad's voice reverberating in my ear. My friends and I had a whole lot in common, but most of them got a chance to experience what it was like to have a father presence. That separated us in terms of them learning how to mimic a man's walk long before I knew what a man actually looked like. They had the things I yearned for the most, and that was a fathers protection, guidance, and the resources that a father brings to the table. Being raised without a father in my life taught me some valuable lessons like:

1. The importance of Dad's presence in his child's life! Men and fathers everywhere must know the devastating effect of leaving their child with inadequate provision, little to no guidance, and unprotected. These contributing factors will strip children of their identity?

2. According to the U.S. Census Bureau, 24 million children in America live in biological father-absent homes. Research

shows when a child grows up in a father-absent home, he or she has the following probabilities.

a. Four Times More Likely to Live in Poverty
b. More Likely to Face Abuse and Neglect
c. More Likely to Suffer Emotional and Behavioral Problems
d. More Likely to Abuse Drugs and Alcohol

Therefore, it's very much necessary to show your child that they are important to you by being directly involved in their lives. If not, your absence will leave a noticeable dint. The former president of National Fatherhood Initiative Roland Warren said "Kids have a hole in their soul in the shape of their Dad. And if a father is unwilling or unable to fill that hole, it can leave a wound that is not easily healed."

Some fathers have abdicated their role and elect not to sit on the throne of responsibility, accountability and commitment. Some are making major decision today that usually end up costing the child more than it would them. So, I strongly urge men to count the cost of having such a huge responsibility enter their life.

3. Understanding the true meaning of *manhood.*

I was totally convinced during my childhood and upbringing that being a womanizer, drinking alcohol, gambling, and hanging in bars would earn me my manhood card. It wasn't until later in life that I discovered that when you live this type of lifestyle it does a great job of breaking your moral reasoning and teaches you how to cover up what has not been fully developed in a man's life. So how does a young man with no consistent male guidance become a man? I am so glad you asked that question. There are several steps to earning your manhood card that has nothing to do with misogyny, or increased health risk. For starters, I will share this with you to grow on and the other lessons will naturally come to you. First, a man must recognize that he can't become a man without a blueprint. You will definitely need a mentor in your life that who naturally illustrates good character in his life daily. If he is the man you think he is then you would easily see traits like: maturity, responsibility, accountability and commitment, etc...

Living an exemplary life requires a man to release some things from his life that he once valued. A good mentor will not only tell you, but show you by example how to live a healthy lifestyle. Second, Kill all your aliases, Mordecai Richler said, a boy can be two, three, four potential people, but a man is only one. He murders the others. You may be sitting there reading this and asking yourself, what is he talking about? Well, I will tell you exactly what I am talking about. Give this some thought for a minute. Some men wear many masks with no conscience before they come to the realization that their life is a counterfeit. Here's an example for you, your buddies like to party all night and now all of sudden you're up all night partying and being a binge drinker except, you do not like the taste of alcohol and you have a job to go to in the morning. You are willing to shape shift into whatever works for acceptance. This is a real good indication that you need to seek for someone that's reputable, to help you to begin the process of building good character. Have the funeral and move on!

The lesson taught at this point by human experience is simply this that the man, who will get up, will be helped up and the man, who will not get up, will be allowed to stay down. Personal independence is a virtue and it is the soul out of which comes the sturdiest manhood. But there can be no independence without a large share of self-dependence, and this virtue cannot be bestowed. It must be developed from within.   – Frederick Douglas

4. It's imperative that you remain **Consistent**

While almost any man can father a child, there is so much more to the important role of being Dad in a child's life. Let's look at a father's role, and why he's irreplaceable. Fathers are central to the emotional well-being of their children; they are capable caretakers, teachers and disciplinarians.

Several studies show that if Dad is affectionate, supportive, and involved, he can contribute greatly to his child's cognitive, language, and social development, as well as academic achievement, a strong inner core, sense of well-being, good self-esteem, and authenticity.

How does this happen for my child? You must establish your presence in your child's life. Some men think home is where you eat, sleep and keep the peace. No! Home is where Dad teaches economic stability by working daily, and where he shows love by giving his children and their mother the unconditional love they so rightly deserve.

How do you remain consistent in your child's life? Well, I believe you must work hard at being reliable for the ones who have the most right to depend on you. Life for a man once he makes a decision to become a father drastically changes for him. Life is no longer solely about you and your needs; it's now about your family and starting that family simply means that you're to become selfless!

The birth of my son totally erased my inherent self-centeredness. I stood firm that I would never have children. I was just too selfish and vain. How could I possibly give to someone else when it was always about me? But life's situations have a way of assisting in one's own personal growth. As my children grew older, I started noticing little changes in me. I begin to see myself attending to their every need, forsaking my own desires. It quickly became not what I wanted, but rather, what they wanted. Of course, I will not sit here and profess to be the perfect parent, but I made it my purpose daily to see life through the same lenses that they were looking out of, which was the key factor of why, even though when their mother and I divorced, I refused to let my children feel the emptiness that I felt growing up without a father.

Some would say you're a good father or you're sacrificing for your child, "Parental sacrifices." However, sacrifice implies that I giving up something so important of value. In truth, an immature

Dad gains so much more from the process of being there for his child—the meaningful cost that we're making will prove to be a substantial difference in the lives of our children. The joy that I feel now seeing my children grown and still learning gives me all the pleasure I need. So, before you make a selfish decision to walk out on your child, understand that they'll feel the effects long after you're gone.

I'll leave you with this thought-

Manhood stretches far past masculinity and the myths of manhood; True manhood is a lifestyle that men must adopt for the improvement of our world. In order for this world to move past it current state of confusion, men must fulfill their purpose such as: stamp out evil as we know it to be so prevalent today, protect their family from falsehoods, provide for their family without thought of their own selfish desires, and provide guidance to their family above everything else, because a house that's divided will not stand!

Sources:

1. *Fathers' Influence in The Lives of Children with Adolescent Mothers. Journal of Family Psychology, 20, 468- 476.* Howard, K. S., Burke Lefever, J. E., Borkowski, J.G., & Whitman, T. L. (2006).
2. (U.S. Census Bureau)
3. (Child's Bureau)
4. (Journal of Marriage and Family

Shon Owens is a humanitarian, father engagement specialist, author, motivational speaker, and mentor

Mr. Shon Owens is currently the coordinator of Aliquippa Council of Men and Fathers/Fatherhood Initiative of Beaver County, an initiative of Franklin Center of Beaver County Inc., in Aliquippa PA.

Mr. Owens was a member of the United States Navy. Mr. Owens is the founder of SJO Ministries Inc. He currently holds the position of Chairman for Beaver County Mental Health/Intellectual Disabilities Board, and serves on the boards of Cultural/Linguistic Competency Advisory Committee, Leaders Serving Beaver County, Family Group Decision Making Advisory Council.

Mr. Owens has coordinated numerous youth projects and events through-out the Tri-State area and has become a recognized leader in the Southwestern PA region. He was recently awarded the 2015 House of Representatives Citation, the 2015 Senate of Pennsylvania Citation, the 2015 Christ's Kingdom Ministry Center Most Influential African-American in the City of Aliquippa, the 2015 Martin Luther King Celebration Committee Community Service Award, 2014 Black Male Engagement Award, the 2014 Deliverance Temple Legacy Award, First Quarter Recipient of the 2012 Franklin Avenue Downtown Award, Fourth Quarter Recipient of the 2010 Franklin Avenue Downtown Award both presented by the Aliquippa Franklin Avenue Development Committee. Other honors include the Church in the Round Men's Ministry Community Leader Appreciation Award, and he is also a recipient of the District Attorney's Community Leader Appreciation Award.

He currently lives very close to Aliquippa in Center Township Pennsylvania with his wife Jikkiko.

Chapter 14

"You Think You Know Everything, Don't You?"
By Dr. Patrick J. Kelly

What lessons have I learned from my parents? That's a loaded question in my world… my upbringing was less than the traditional nuclear family. Suffice to say, in retrospect, I wouldn't have had it any other way. What I did have was a loving network of caregivers, which were for the most part, my extended family from both maternal and paternal sides. The key component to my extended parental sphere was simple…love! They all had different paths…some chose the road less traveled, some were more predictable…but the underlying direction was neatly intertwined with the same destination in mind.

My most influential father figure was my mother, my single mother, who was on her own with not much help…if any help from my father…in my early years. We were very poor and she struggled to make ends meet. I do not remember much time in my life that she did not work at least two jobs and sometimes three. This story is nothing new, millions of families struggle in poverty. What is important about our poverty while I was a child was my utter ignorance of our situation. Not just poverty, but a *myriad* of statistical detriments that I choose not to discuss at this time, but should have included me in their numbers. Why did I escape becoming just another statistic? Because of what I learned from my mother…

I learned unconditional love. Growing up, I cannot remember a day that I didn't feel like I was the most important thing in my mother's life. Her love affirmed my self-worth…a feeling that I was deserving of love…deserving of a great life.

I witnessed sacrifice. One of the primary reasons I was oblivious to our poverty was my mother's sacrifices. She went without so I didn't have to. Oddly enough, looking back she spoiled me. Something I as an adult pre-father frowned upon. Those kids, spoiled brats…unappreciative of what was bestowed upon them I thought to myself. As a father now, I realize the true art of parenting she possessed was the gift of spoiling me until the moment I felt entitled or worthy of something I didn't earn…and instantly put me in my place. You see, I learned at an early age that hard work is rewarded. She wasn't spoiling me…she was rewarding me for hard work or an accomplishment…something I *earned*.

This is a perfect segue into the next attribute she instilled in me. I learned tenacity and work ethic. As an example, I was not nagged to get good grades. I felt it was just what was normal, that I expected of myself. I learned to be humble; I never touted my accomplishments…sometimes to the dismay of my mother. Two memories stick out in my head on this topic. The first was when I was asked to be the altar boy by our priest on the local televised mass. She came home from work the next day and asked me if I was on TV serving mass? She was upset that a co-worker told her she saw me the morning before on TV serving mass. I affirmed, and she asked why I didn't tell her? I told her I didn't think it was a big deal. The first time I got a 4.0 GPA…ditto. She read it in the paper. You can probably guess I was not rewarded for good grades and such. I was rewarded for things that made good grades seem inconsequential to me. I was rewarded for things that are the foundation for working hard…getting good grades or other accolades are the by-product of these lessons. These core values were what I was praised for.

Responsibility was one of those values and it was learned early in life. I am embarrassed to share this story…but it is true. While I was in grade school (I believe second grade) my mother left for work long before I had to leave to catch the bus for school. This unfortunate "free time" was frequently used to sleep...and miss my bus to school. I'm not embellishing, but I missed the bus a lot. The crux of this issue came to a head one week that I had missed the bus for the third time in one week during the peak of winter. I made the dreaded call to my mother's work for the third time that week. I could hear the anger, disappointment, and helplessness in her voice as she knew she had to call for back-up yet again this week... The last thing she said before she hung up was "if you don't get to school, I'm going to kill you!" Did I think she would kill me? Hell no! Did I think she was going to hurt me in any way? Hell no! Did I think I think I let her down? Yes! Dropped the ball? Yes! Pilfered my responsibility? Yes! That's why I will never forget the details of this story... right down to my mom's voice over the phone, the sweat running down my face as I ran, the tan and red corduroy jacket I was wearing, the brisk chill of the dead of winter, the gloves and hat I was *not* wearing, the gratuitous amount of snow on the shoulders of the road (it was a back country road, not sidewalks and such), the silence...all I could hear was the beating of my heart echoing in my head, how alone I felt with my thoughts and regrets, the ridiculous distance from my house to the school... about three miles, and did I mention the amount of trouble I was in for missing the bus again.

The real story began when I arrived at the school late, sweaty, and scared... I will never forget the reaction of the nuns. "My God child what happened to you?" As a child, of course I responded with purity and honesty... "My mom told me she would kill me if I didn't get to school, so I ran here." In retrospect, for me, this is the moment where you walk into a room and you hear the needle scratch off the record and go silent!

The nuns called my mom at work and asked her about the situation...I was there in the room and heard the response. Of course I told him I would kill him. He missed the bus for the third time this week...wouldn't you have wanted to kill him? The moral of the story...was I in danger? No, she was obviously speaking figuratively, not literally. I went home to my loving mother who was more scared than I was over the ordeal. So if this had happened today...I would have never made it home that day after school. The nuns could have called child protective services...my how times have changed! On to the next one...

Tenacity was another value. It was ok to not be good at something or not being able to do something. What was not acceptable was to give up...stop trying to do things you are passionate about. I learned respect...for my elders, others, and myself.

I learned fear. Fear of my mother. I mean this in the most positive of ways. I was afraid to disappoint her, let her down. I feared my punishment if I played the fool. Punishment is a touchy subject...not in my opinion...but apparently in the media, schools, social media, and at social gatherings. In today's day and age, parents are judged by their choice of punishment. In my opinion, I gained perspective on the subject at an early age. There is not a one size fits all solution for disciplining our children. Early on my mom used to "beat my butt" which was not effective on me. Apparently she learned that one time when I told her to "just beat me and get it over with." What we also learned together was that grounding me...from outside play time or specific toys was much more effective. In essence, I did learn that discipline is dependent on personality, circumstances, and stages of development.

In my opinion, the personal emotional pain of doing something wrong before the child ever faces punishment is the best discipline. That awful feeling in your stomach...everyone has experienced that emotional torment of guilt...regret...remorse. Unless you are dealing with a sociopath, this is the learned response to breaking the rules. Rules of your home, society, relationships, and work, these are only a few. What does your child realize as the most pungent form of discipline? Which has consistently produced the best behavior?

I wish it was simple; unfortunately, the rules change over the developmental stages of some children. As a youngster, where physical punishment was ineffective and grounding (loss of privileges) was effective...as a teen, the emotional punishment became the bane of my existence. The earliest example of this that I can remember was at the age of thirteen, it was my response to the question "You think you know everything, don't you?" To which my response was, "Just about." I'm not sure the "t" in "about" was fully expressed into the ether before my face was slapped opened handed...for the first time in my life. Thank you, mom, for helping me to realize how insolent I was; and, that I deserved that. I was so embarrassed to have acted like such an arrogant ass and disrespected my mother...that it truly bothered me. That was my punishment. The "motivation" was not to feel the disappointment for letting myself and others down. The deterrent was not the physical slap.

Looking back, other parental figures seemed like a clandestine group of operatives charged with assuring my success and survival. They all seemed to have their specific roles in the shaping of my personality. There are not words to describe my love and admiration for these people. My gratitude for all the physical, financial, and emotional support can never be repaid, nor is it expected. I will do my best to pass on their life lessons and love throughout my life as my repayment.

Aunt Patty and Uncle Rick specialized in unconditional love. My paternal grandfather specialized in being strict...the consummate northern Irishman. His specialty was grammar and everything else that was mundane. I mean this in the purest form of admiration...he paid attention to details...and made sure I did as well. Uncle Danny, aka "Crazy Uncle Tenuse" was a crazy version of grand pap. Think a cross between Hunter Stockton Thompson and Jack Kerouac. From him I witnessed the perils of excess and the need for self-restraint…that need was desperately needed by more than a few on my father's side. Ultimately, from him, I learned to not judge a book by its cover. He looked…well crazy! Think Sadam Hussein when they captured him in that hole… He is one of the most eccentric and intelligent people I know. He taught me knowledge matters. My other uncles taught me that the nuclear family really can exist. They are/were great men with successful careers and strong family values. I always had strong admiration for them and their achievements. My paternal grandmother, well she specialized in criticism…of everyone but me. Apparently, this is a Lebanese maternal trait. Lastly, I had five Lebanese great aunts. God bless them…all but one made everything serious and about learning. Aunt Yvonne thanks for the eternal smile and showing the lighter side of "the house." That was the family name for the home of all the spinster great aunts that was the center of the family, especially around the holidays.

My maternal grandparents were much different. For starters, I had three great grandparents for the majority of my life, the last surviving into my thirties. They were of Irish and Polish descent…my God…more Irish influence! With very little interaction on the subject of being grateful…for some reason this was the greatest lesson I learned from them. Perhaps it had to do with me being a curious child and constantly wanting to know what it was like when they were little. I wanted to know what it was like to not have a phone…and things relevant to their childhood. I guess hearing about how little they had…of necessities, let alone luxuries made me feel grateful for what I had. Maybe there is something to the old adage "I walked five miles in the snow to school with no shoes, and it was uphill both ways!"

My grandmother, on the other hand, taught me that everything will be o.k. Even when it wasn't going to be okay; she helped me understand that it's o.k. to not be o.k.! She always acted as if she didn't have a care in the world. Her name was Dorothy and everyone called her Dot or Dory. Her nick name from the family was "Hunky Dory" because of her carefree attitude. My aunts and uncles on my mother's side were comfort. Her family was close for the most part. I was always happy with them. I could always just be myself and know I was loved and accepted—a feeling every child deserves.

My grandfather, he was more of a disciplinarian...but by no means strict or overbearing. Things were pretty lenient when I stayed there. He taught me one of the most valuable lessons in my life, Happiness, regardless of the situation. His situation was pretty grim. He persevered through five leg amputations. No he was not an arachnid or some other unearthly creature...he had three amputations on one of his legs and two on the other. They occurred over several years as they tried to preserve as much of each leg as possible. During one of the surgeries his left arm suffered nerve damage from the way it was positioned during surgery, and it never recovered. So there he was, one leg amputated above the knee, one just below the knee, and a bunk left arm. He had severe phantom pain for which they could not find a remedy...so he was in chronic never ending pain. Through the years and with his conditions I never saw him unhappy unless I walked into the room unexpectedly...and saw him rubbing his stumps with a horrid grimace of pain on his face. At times I would watch for a few seconds before I announced my presence...to see if it was a fleeting shot of pain or a lasting pain with a longer duration. Not once did I see him stop until I said his name or made some noise so he knew I was there. He instantly stopped the grimace and smiled...every time. He had every reason to be unhappy all the time...but wasn't. He may have been in pain at times but he sure wasn't unhappy. He had a routine; he drove with a modified vehicle. He had a life and did things. He did not dwell on his misfortune; he made the best of his situation. I always tell myself...to this day...if "Robopap" (my nick name for him because of his prosthetic legs and electrolarynx) could be happy, then there should never be a reason for me to be unhappy with any situation life presents to me. Did I mention he had throat cancer and couldn't speak without his vibrating thing he held to his throat? He rarely used it. I learned happiness is not based on circumstances, good or bad. I learned it is a choice from him. One of my favorite sayings I have for people in turmoil and distress is "I've woke up with more than I knew what to do with and I've woke up with nothing...What I learned from those moments, regardless of the situation, was when I woke in the morning I felt the same...happy." My circumstances were not the determining factor in my happiness or lack of it.

Sometimes role models are found in the darndest of places. The "godfather" of my boys...undeniably the best father who has not yet had kids...taught me that all family does not come from a bloodline. His selfless acts over the years have left me humbled and we are lucky to have him be a part of the boys' lives. Jett and Rocco will be better men because of his caring nature and sage advice to both the boys and myself. Great advice has come from some golf buddies...who ended up becoming great friends. The majority are my seniors by twenty-five to thirty years or more. I have a penchant for a fellow Irishman that I can confide in for advice. Then there are the Italians...suffice to say, I have a lot of friends... I cannot say enough how important it is to seek advice from people you love and trust that have been down that road before. I make mention of nationalities for no other reason than the differences in family dynamics from culture to culture that I have noticed that surprise and intrigue me. It made me have a greater appreciation for my heritage in some way. In my line of work, I see a lot of people on a weekly basis, socially as well as in my work environment. I am thankful for their friendship and advice on a regular basis.

What have I learned from my father? I never want my boys to feel the sadness and disappointment of not having me around. I saddled that pain for the majority of my life...and will into the future. He was quite a character, when asked about my father…from acquaintances I had a standard response. "Poppa was a rolling stone." I loved and admired him for all the attributes that made him a great person and entrepreneur. I spent a lifetime learning to let go of the pain and disappointment he caused. The dynamics of our relationship would require a book of its own, so we will leave that story for another day.

What have I learned from *being* a father? I would extend the question to what I have learned from being part of a loving family? I learned that as awesome as it was to grow up with an amazing mother…it is even more awesome to watch my wife, Nicolina, be an inspirational and loving mother to our two boys Jett and Rocco. What have I learned…that dreams do come true! My sincerest thanks to family and friends for what you gave to me; love and inspiration through the years.

Dr. Patrick J. Kelly completed his undergraduate studies at the University of Pittsburgh and received his Doctorate of Chiropractic from Palmer College of Chiropractic West. He has been in private practice since educating his patients about healthier lifestyles through diet, exercise, and chiropractic care.

Dr. Kelly's passion for the Chiropractic Profession can be seen through his tireless efforts working with state and national associations for years to improve the quality and access of Chiropractic care. Dr. Kelly is a past President of the Pennsylvania Chiropractic Association (PCA), as well as numerous other leadership positions in the PCA. He was voted Chiropractor of the Year by his peers in 2008.

Along with Private practice, Dr. Kelly is also the Chief Medical Officer of Elite Science, a nutraceutical company. Dr. Kelly has also designed an Electronic Health Records cloud based computer system for use in chiropractic offices. He has been published professionally in the chiropractic profession. He now has his sights set on becoming an aspiring author of children's books.

Dr. Kelly's pride and joy is his family, his lovely wife Nicolina and his two boys Jett and Rocco. He is a passionate father who does his best to raise his boys with values he learned growing up. Family time is cherished time spent together regardless of the activity.

Dr. Kelly enjoys many hobbies, most which he can share with his Family. He is an avid golfer, snowboarder, and cyclist. He also has a deep interest in physics and how its laws affect our daily lives. He has a firm belief that the next great things to happen to our civilization will come from a better understanding of the laws of quantum mechanics and that kids should be exposed to it early in life through every day concepts they can relate to.

To learn more about Dr. Kelly, his books, and his blogs, visit his website doctordaddysaidso.com.

Dads' Exercise: What are myths and truths about Fatherhood?

- Babies sleep all the time: Newborns sleep a lot – typically up to 16 to 17 hours a day. But most babies don't stay asleep for more than two to four hours at a time, day or night, during the first few weeks of life.

- What I do doesn't matter: Researchers have found that parenting styles can influence child development outcomes. For example, children raised by authoritative parents tend to grow up to be happy and capable while those raised by permissive parents tend to have more problems with authority figures and are less successful in school.

- Parents are too involved: Children with parents who respond quickly to their needs and play more with their kids tend to have secure attachment styles. Kids with this style of attachment tend to be more empathetic, have stronger self-esteem, and are more mature than children with other attachment styles.

- Discipline is a bad thing: The authoritative parenting style is often identified as the best style overall. This style is more likely to produce children who are competent, confident, and happy. Parents with this style of parenting listen to their children and provide warmth and support, but provide limits, expectations, and consequences for behavior.Feeling bad about daycare: While parents often worry about leaving their children at daycare or with a babysitter, developmental psychologists believe that such child care can be a positive influence on a child as long as it is of high quality. By being selective and watching out for any potential warning signs, parents can help ensure that their children receive the best possible care.

- Children see too much violence: Sixty percent of American children were exposed to violence, crime, or abuse in their homes, schools, and communities. - 2009 Department of Justice Study.

- Only my child acts out: According to research for National Teething Week, 68 per cent of parents have left a public place because of a crying child.

- My child knows better, we do not need to talk about sex: Three (3) in 10 teen American girls will get pregnant at least once before age 20. That's nearly 750,000 teen pregnancies every year.

Chapter 15

Do Dads Cry Too?
By Anthony S. Fludd Sr.

It all began 12-03-93. I left Bedstuy "Do or Die" Brooklyn, New York. I left behind all 3 of my mothers, Ethel, Mary and Roslyn. Each one played an intricate part in raising and guiding me after my biological mom died. I was 5 years old when she died. I don't remember anything about her. The only thing I remember is having 3 Moms. Although my head was as hard as a brick, and I never followed their rules, they never stopped loving me. To this day, I thank each one of them for supporting and loving my siblings Tyrone, Marrion and I as their own. My Father was around, but not around. I don't put all the blame on him, nor do I have any animosity towards him, because him not being around forced me to grow up. I learned how to fight from the streets; I learned all about the ladies from the street, I learned to tie a tie from the streets. I guess this was God's plan for me. I had to go through my process, my journey to find out my purpose.

20 years later, I was a father of 4 Kings. My oldest got his driver's license when he was 16. I bought him his first car shortly after. A few months later he was in his first accident and my second child, born Aaron, was in the car as well. Nothing is worse than almost losing a child, but the feeling is 10 times worse when it's nearly two.

Two weeks after the crash my eight-year-old son walked up on me as I was writing an entry in my journal. I was unprepared for the interruption and my eyes were filled with tears and red. He asked, "Dad, are you okay?" I immediately tried to be SuperDad and put on a brave face wiping my eyes and said yes I'm okay as if to suggest all was well and that I was simply rubbing my tired eyes, but he was discerning and knew better. I could tell by his expression he knew I was grieving. In that moment, I thought to myself what good do I do for my children when I pretend. I realized I do them no favors when I'm not being real. At that moment, I looked him in the eyes and said, "Actually I'm not okay, but I am okay, do you know what I mean?" Relief washed over his face and I could tell he not only understood, but that he was glad I was being real—as if it gave him permission to be real too. I want my children to know that it is okay to hurt, that you can be okay, but not okay and that's okay.

He and I talked about Uncle Richard for a while and he shared some of his sorrows about losing Uncle Richard, Rose and others. We both cried together I hugged him and let him know how much I love him every bit as much. We crossed a major bridge with grief that day. My son knew it was okay to hurt and pretending otherwise serves nobody, not even ourselves. To the contrary we do a great disservice when we pretend.

When Rose died a few years prior, I read the words of an 18th-century French writer who wrote.... We discover in ourselves what others hide from us and we recognize in others what we hide from ourselves. When I read those words I vowed to retire my SuperDad mask and be real. I tried to have similar exchanges with my other children. My children each uniquely process their grief differently and that's okay too. In all things, I want to be real with them...for it is when we're real that we become equipped to deal with real life. I realized I cannot run from sorrow anymore than I can run from my shadow on a sunny day. I must learn to live with love and sorrow and understand that, "I'm okay, but I'm not okay, and that's okay."

I know you are probably wondering who's Rose. Well Rose was my Fourth mother. When I took that Greyhound ride to DC in 1993, Rose and her children Lorenzo and Dedra welcomed me with open arms. We became a family. She was my new Mom and they were my new brother and sister. My other brother and sister later moved down with us. My sister Marrion soon gave birth to her first born. He was born with a cone head, we named him Devon. That was my street name growing up in Brooklyn. My fourth mother, Rose, was murdered by her husband. He beat her to death. This by far was the most devastating event my family and I had ever gone through. I've gone to several funerals in my life but this one was the toughest. The only way I could deal and cope was to speak at her funeral. We wrote a poem about how she loved to cook and sing. And everyone smiled and laughed. When it was time to put her in that ground next to my biological Mom, Grandma and my other family everyone wanted to jump right in there with her. It was hard, she was loved and she's still loved.

But let me tell you what God did for me, God Sent a Princess to patch my heart. I didn't think I could make a girl. I thought my genes were too manly. But once again God had a plan for me. He knew I was missing a piece in my heart after my Fourth Mother's death, so he gave me a DaddyDoll. I wrote her this poem I plan to read at her wedding one day.

"My first ain't my first; she's a little girl to a recycled Dad. I had no idea then it dawned on me, this diaper don't have what the rest had.

It was so strange to look and see, this DaddyDoll belonged to me. I had no idea how to be, as I feared nothing would come natural to me.

With her tiny body upon my chest I quickly got her dressed, I had no idea my DaddyDoll, would have a bone that looked like breast.

Those that know me well have wondered who'll have it worst. I'm pretty sure Barack and Jay Z have also purchased a hearse.

I don't plan to shake his hand when he shows up to take her to the school dance. I'll simply place my hand on his shoulder and whisper you got one chance.

I'll sit thru dance recitals or fashion shows even if I was the only one there, I'll clap with the enthusiasm of a thousand people and assure you to have no fear.

But if you choose touchdowns or layups which is habitual for me, I'll be walking up the sideline shaking my head at the referee.

Time flies fast and I have no Idea where it goes, you'll soon be saying farewell to dollies, blankies and bows.

Then comes the day I'm welcomed to makeup, telephones and boys, just keep in mind this shiny piece of metal, ain't one of your brothers toys."

Eighteen months after my DaddyDolls birth I'm now known as the Father of four Kings and one Queen. I also have a Niece, Christenel, I call her my DauNeice. She's like my Daughter, but my Niece. I soon learned that life as a parent had two huge transitions. The first is when they arrive and the second when they leave. It was time for my First born son to leave for college at Morgan State University and my DauNeice was leaving for the U.S. Army.

Moments like this give us parents one-time opportunities to say things to our children that will stick with them not only because of what we said, but because of when it is said. However in the end our job as a parent is to leave them with both the right size sheets and a sense that they are well equipped for this next independent stage of life. This goes to prove that when they are little they sit in your lap, once they grow up they sit on your heart.

As a Father I live for moments like this. Later that year my first born son won his first NCAA Division 1 Football MEAC Championship Ring and my DauNeice graduated from basic training and advance individual training. Once again I was a proud Dad and thankful to be blessed with great children. Not only were the older children making me proud the younger were as well. My second born son Aaron was a stand-out Student-Athlete. He consistently maintained a 3.7 GPA and played on the 2015 Maryland State 4A Football Championship team for Dr. Henry Wise High School. He also brought a ring home.

My third born son, Andrew, whom consistently maintained a 3.8 GPA never failed to make me a proud parent by having the opportunity to attend his Honor Roll ceremony for the billionth time in a row as well as publicly speaking in front of senate committees to change Maryland laws to support shared parenting. He too will soon go on to be a successful Student-Athlete. I wouldn't trade the world for any of the experiences my children have blessed me with, good or bad.

Despite all the success my children blessed me with, I soon found myself in the midst of a Custody/Visitation case in the Family Court for over a year. As of January 2016, I haven't seen my youngest two for an entire year. This felt very much like the feelings I had when my oldest two were in the accident. It hurts more than words can explain. I went from being an involved father every day, to not seeing them at all. I continued to say to myself, "I'm ok, but I'm not ok, but that's ok." I have faith and I pray and I pray, but I cry and I cry. What some fail to admit is that Dads Cry Too! Those tears are cleansing tears. It's God's way of cleansing your body of the hurt and pain.

It's God's way of saying, "Hold on, help is on the way." So, I won't give up. I will continue to fight for my children's right to have a meaningful relationship with BOTH their parents. I soon realized that this fight for my children's rights was very much like the fight for civil rights. In no way shape or form should this be considered harassing to anyone. Was it harassing when Susan B. Anthony fought for Women's Suffrage? Was it harassing when Dr. Martin Luther King Jr. fought for civil rights, and was it harassing when Edward McNamara did everything he could for seven years to seek a relationship with his daughter who was born in 1981 to a San Diego woman who had given her up for adoption, following a brief affair?

This was not about a conflict with the mother of my children. I'm simply not a father who is willing to except being labeled as an "unknown", "unavailable" or "uninterested" unwed BabyDaddy. I'm the Father of four Kings and one Queen and I believe that children are a cherished gift from the God—and that both parents are primarily responsible for guiding and preparing them for a life of service to God and to humanity.

I share this message with you with hopes to inspire someone to not give up on life and to continue to fight for your children. Many men commit suicide after dealing with the stress and depression from losing their wife, house, job and/or children.

While I realize it's hard, I ask that you put God first and become selfless. Use your mess as a message to help someone else. The most selfless thing you can do in this world is help someone else.

It's selfless because of the gratification and the goodness that comes to you from helping others. Nothing is better than that. That's where the joy is. Selfless means putting someone else's needs above your own. Acting selflessly isn't easy, but the more you practice the better you'll get at being kind and generous more often. When you make a habit of taking action to help others and making the world a better place, you'll see that being selfless can actually make you happier. Remember in order for God to do something for you, you gotta do something for others.

Fight for your family. A sign you're headed in the right direction is when you have opposition. If the devil isn't trying to stop you then you're not doing anything worth doing. In the midst of opposition, critics, fault finders, and people who can't encourage you and just talk about you, keep praying. You'll realize when you begin to pray and make the right choices, you're going to begin to see yourself halfway to where you wanted to go.

Don't let fear direct your choices. Fear is a satanic tactic. Always move in the direction of your fears. Don't be afraid. We serve a God who has already demonstrated how awesome and great he is. Don't quit, don't give up. Fight for your families, sons and daughters.

Anthony Jr., Aaron, Andrew, Ayden and Alexandra You'll always be my four Kings and one Queen. I love all my family, supporters and friends and I will treat anyone's child like my own, Tiffany, Kasey, Thomas, Jasmine, Javon, Devon, Christenel, Brian, James, Delonte, Kendra, Tyrese, Donte Jr., Tyler, Jordan, and last but not least Emmanuel, although some of you are grown now, I'll always love you all like my own and remember I'm ok, but I'm not ok, but that's ok. To be continued...

I LOVE MY 5 A'S!!!!!!

Anthony Fludd Sr. is a native of Bedford Stuyvesant (Do or Die) Brooklyn New York and has lived in Prince Georges County Maryland since 1993.

Anthony is a proud Father of 4 boys and 1 girl. His background and focus on community collaboration began in 1996 as a volunteer with the local Boys and Girls Club in Prince Georges County. Anthony retired from the U.S. Army in 2008. Following his retirement Anthony took on a number of community leadership roles such as coaching sports and/or mentoring. Through Anthony's experiences growing up he utilized his story as a message for many youth. In 2012 Anthony founded the organization, Positive People Against Domestic Abuse, but later changed the name to Dads Cry Too.

The organization has afforded Anthony an opportunity to organize around many issues such as youth development, domestic violence and parental rights. One of the main goals Anthony seeks is to bring awareness and resources to the community regarding Fathers rights and domestic violence. Anthony stands firm in his believe that EVERY CHILD has a right to have a meaningful relationship with BOTH parents. "I LOVE MY 5 A's"

Go Ask Your Dad

Chapter 16

Who Do You Talk to in The Coffee Shop?
By Al Latronica

Our days would start at the coffee shop. My father would order a cup of coffee and an old-fashioned donut. He would set his cup in front of him and add in just the right amount of cream, so it was just the right color, not too dark, not too light. He would slowly stir the coffee, as he contemplated his next move. Then he would open up a napkin, lay it neatly next to his cup and place his old-fashion donut down on the napkin. It was the only kind he ever ate. He said it was the perfect donut, plan, sweet and it worked well with his coffee. He would then break the doughnut in half, and then in half again, so there would be four equal quarters. He would pick up one quarter and dunk it into the coffee, just enough to get a bit of the coffee into the small nooks and crannies of the doughnut. Then he would take a bite, sit quietly for a moment and savored the taste. Only then a lesson would begin.

My father was an Italian immigrant from southern Italy. When my grandmother was pregnant with my father, my grandfather sent her to the United States so he could be born here, and be a US citizen. With the political changes in Italy, this was important to many immigrating families. She took the boat back and forth from Italy to the US three more times with both of my uncles and my aunt. Finally, in the mid-30s, the entire family moved to the United States permanently. When they arrived my grandfather had to find work. He had some experience in the building trades, so it made sense to find a job in the construction business. And as it happens so often, that became the trade of my dad and his brothers. It was difficult for my father and his family.

They did not speak English very well, so fitting in and learning the customs was difficult. My father would tell me stories about how he and his brothers were teased and bullied when going to school. He would tell me how some days they would have to fight just to get through the day. While my uncles continued to use their fist to settle disputes, my father found a better way, a quite way. Still, my father and his brothers had to find an outlet for their frustration, find a way to fit in. Then they discovered the game of football and as it turned out, they were very good athletes. Entering high school in the mid-40s, this made them popular with the school, and not surprising, making it easier for them to assimilate into the population. It ended that my father and his brothers became the top football athletes during that time in Pittsburgh. It gave them opportunities that many young immigrants did not have. It gave them the opportunity, through football, to attend college.

Attending college was a difficult decision to make for the family, the boys were needed back home to work. My grandfather could not see the value of college, so he did not instill the need for continued education into his children. It wasn't that my grandfather did not want great things for his kids, but in many instances his hands were tied. That just wasn't the way of the world then. My father had the opportunity to go to college on a football scholarship, but chose the Marine Corps instead. A few years later my uncle became the number one recruited high school athlete in the country for football. He had offers to over 100 colleges. He went to play at Michigan State, but left shortly after he arrived deciding he knew more than the coach. He and my dad never did go to college. So it was back to work, get married and start to raise a family. It didn't take my father long to realize that not taking the opportunity to get a college education was a mistake. He knew that if life was going to be better for his children, college wasn't an option. We were going.

This became somewhat of a mantra for my dad. He would tell

me when my brothers and sister and I were little that every day he would come home from work, pick us up and tell us how much he loved us, and told us we were going to college. Going to college meant everything to him. He recognized that by going to college we could have things better than him. Isn't that what it's all about? Creating a life for your children by teaching them the lessons they need to learn so their lives could be better than yours.

It seems like we have lost some of that in our modern times, with all the distractions. We believe we have the answers at our finger tips by simply asking google or siri. The need for immediacy has made our organic conversations mute. We seem to find that the dialogue of what is going to make our children better has changed somehow. The message then was simple, be patient, work hard and you can achieve what you want to achieve in life. I don't think the message has changed, but maybe the messenger has.

So, growing up in a construction family in Pittsburgh Pennsylvania, in the 50s, 60s, and 70s was not easy. You see, for me, back then, Pittsburgh was about three things; steel, construction and football. In my family all three of those things seem to work together. The way it worked was this. During the hay-days of the steel mills in Pittsburgh, the mills employed a great number of workers, and jobs were plentiful. The coal mining in that area also produced a great number of jobs because they supplied the fuel for the mills. The steel mills created the product that was sold to the world so people could make a good income, and live a great life in Pittsburgh. This gave the opportunity for those of us in the construction family to build houses, repair houses, and in general have plenty of work to make a great living in that business as well.

As I mentioned football was an important part of our lives then as well. We will get back to that. Then came the 1960s. Freedom, "The Revolution", Vietnam, and the beginning of the collapse of our post war thriving economy. The steel mills began to shut down because the world was not interested in American steel. One by one as the mills began to close, the need for coal became less and less, so the mines closed as well. With nobody making money from the mines or the mills the construction business began to fail. I remember a lot of very lean times growing up.

One very vivid memory that I have was is when I was 6 years old. Things were getting very difficult; no work meant my father didn't make any money. Luckily, my uncle worked for the VA, and he had an opportunity to provide for us some surplus food. The food came in the way of large brown bags of flour and rice. It also came in the way of large silver cans that contained spam. We lived in a small two bedroom twin with my dad, my mom, and my two brothers and me, and, oh yeah, our dog Shep. I remember when my uncle first started to bring the food to our house. I would watch my mom open the bags of flour to make bread and pasta. She would use the rice to cook some very inventive meals for our dinners. And because we could not afford dog food, I watch my mother open up the big silver cans of Spam and feed it to the Shep.

Come wintertime my father had no work at all, things got even worse financially for our family. On this one particularly cold winter day, I watched my mother open up a big silver can assuming she was going to feed Shep. What she did instead was begin to slice the spam and put it in the frying pan. The next thing I recall, it was on a plate in the middle of the dinner table. I remember sitting at the table, just staring at the plate. I remember feeling scared, not knowing what to do or say. I was young, but I knew things were not right. When my mom put some of the fried spam on my plate, I just began to cry. When my mother asked me why I was crying, I asked her why did we have to eat dog food. A lot of things changed for our family that day, and my father knew this could not be our future.

So enters a way for us to go to college… football. It turns out that my brothers and I, like my father and his brothers before us, were very good football players. Now my dad knew that this was a means to an end, and the end was a college education. So his job was to instill in us the lessons that we needed in order to make our way into college and a better life. So through football we learned the lessons, much like the lessons we learned on the construction site. We learned to plan our work, work hard at our plan, and always work as a crew, or a team.

This would allow us to complete the job with greater efficiency. And that sounds to me a lot like a football team. In order to win a football game, you make up plays, your plans, you work hard with you teammates to make the plan work, and you achieve your goal of winning the game! Football, construction, and life—how about that?

So from that day forward we worked every weekend, holidays and summers with my dad. He couldn't afford to hire labor so it was us. It was good… We spent time together, time with our dad, and we learned to take a job from the planning stage to completion. We learned to work as a team. Do our job well and the job will be done well. Always support your co-worker or teammate. Be patient. Waking up and going to work in the morning seems to be difficult for some people. It's as easy for me to do now is it was back then. Back when I was younger, I was going to work with my dad, to learn a lesson, complete a job and be proud of our accomplishments. Today, I go to work as a dad and the goal is the same.

I went on to college and played football. Then, I went on to get my doctorate degree. During the time between completing undergrad and going to do my doctorate studies I had the opportunity, the privilege, of working with my dad full-time for about one year. It was just him and me! It was the greatest year of my life.

I opened my private practice on January 1st 1989. My father never got the chance to see my practice; he died of a heart condition March 17th 1989. He was 61 years old. Without him it would have never happened .There is not a day that goes by that I don't miss him. I miss his quiet; I miss his gentle smile, and miss the way he would teach. So many times I didn't know it was a lesson.

Very often we learn without knowing that we are learning. But there was always a lesson. Sometimes the lesson was on patience; sometimes it was on just how to handle a situation the right way. Sometimes it was just conversation and in that conversation you learn something. There doesn't always have to be a beginning, or an end. There doesn't always have to be a conclusion. Sometimes that is the lesson.

If I have to pick one important lesson, of all I have learned, it would have to be patience. If we are patient with ourselves, the answers will come. We have the answers already if we just listen to all the things that come our way from our parents, mentors, and family, the answers are there.

I've come to a time in my life that my children are older, out of college and on their life's path. I hope I used the lessons that I've learned, and was as good at conveying my lessons to my children as my father was for me. With patience, understanding, I hope I instilled in them the idea that they can have what they want. Just dream your dream, work hard, and be patient. But I know there are many more lessons. Many for me to learn and to teach, and I don't always have the answers.

So on those days when I have difficulty making a decision, those days I just can't get it right or I just don't have the right answer, on those days, I go to the coffee shop.

I order a cup of coffee and an old-fashioned donut. I set my cup in front of me and add in just the right amount of cream, so it is just the right color, not too dark, not too light. I slowly stir the coffee, as I contemplate my next move. Then I open up a napkin, I lay it neatly next to my cup and place my old-fashioned donut down on the napkin. It's the only kind he ever ate, the perfect donut, the donut I also eat. I break the doughnut in half, and then in half again, so there would be four equal quarters. I pick up one quarter and dunk it into the coffee, just enough to get a bit of the coffee into the small nooks and crannies of the doughnut. Then I take a bite, sit quietly for a moment and savor the taste. And then, I have a conversation with my dad.

Dr. Al Latronica received his Bachelor of Arts degree from Clarion University. He went on to receive his Doctorate of chiropractic from Life University in Atlanta, Georgia. He is currently in practice in Furlong, Pennsylvania. Dr. Al has been in practice for 30 years and his passion has led him to develop a strong sports and wellness practice. Along with private practice Dr. Al is also the chief medical Director for Performtech International.

Dr. Al is also currently an adjunct professor of Anatomy and Physiology at Bucks College.

Dr. Al has always had a passion for teaching. He has had the opportunity to lecture across the country, on all subjects related to wellness and sports in the chiropractic world. Dr. Al began his career in the sports world by developing a travel to treat chiropractic base treatment protocol for the NFL. This work allowed him the opportunity to work with many professionals in many different professions. Some of his patients include greats like Joe Montana, Jerry Rice, and Charles Haley from the NFL. He has also had the opportunity to work with Arnold Schwarzenegger, tennis greats Evon Lendl and Michael Chang, and cycling great Lance Armstrong. This experience has made Dr. Al a sought after lecturer and program developer in his field.

Dr. Al has had the opportunity to work with the Pennsylvania Chiropractic Association on many different levels of leadership. He was the past president and chairman of the board, and voted chiropractor of the year by his peers in 2012. He continues to work with his state and local associations to educate families on wellness. His hobbies include rugby, basketball, fishing, and anything that takes him outdoors.

Of all the things that Dr. Al has done, his greatest passion is his family. His wife, Pamela, his four children; Stephanie, Danielle, Brittney and Anthony have always been, and will continue to be, the driving force behind his success. His passion for family has allowed him to work his way from the NFL and NBA greats to the minor and midget leagues in order to take his expertise the local to family.

Go Ask Your Dad

Chapter 17

How Am I Designed?
By Tommy Jones

When I was asked to be part of this great project, my first thought was how could I help another man learn to be a great father when I, myself, have not always been a great father? Several years ago, I became a mentor for men within our church because my men's group leaders convinced me I would be good at it. What? Me, a broken man, was leading other men during their time of need? As crazy as that sounds, yes, a broken man leading other men is a great idea. Why? Because someone who is broken or been to a point of brokenness has been comforted, loved, mentored, and taught how to be better. After all, if being a great father was easy, then wouldn't every dad be a great father? To be a great father, doesn't mean we have to have everything figured out or have never done stupid things.

A great mentor and man in my life, John Woodall, has a saying he refers to a lot. He says, "We live and die by our definitions." That is so true, isn't it? Think about your definition of a father for a minute and don't refer to the internet. Just think about the word father. The common definition is the male parent of a child. Maybe some people would say the male parent who has certain legal rights and obligations to their child. According to Wikipedia, a father is defined as the male parent of a (human) child who has a paternal bond with his children, a parental social and legal relationship with his children that carries certain rights and obligations. Does this mean any male adult or man who has a child with a woman can be defined as a father? Sure, but what about a great father? The answer is no. To be a great father, a man can't simply uphold his legal and parental obligations. It takes a lot more than that.

I grew up with two loving parents who pretty much provided me with everything I wanted to some degree. I played different sports and they would take me to practice, games, races, etc. My mother had meals on the table most nights or we ate out. They had us in church for several years and tried to explain the importance of the church. If I needed clothes or shoes, somehow I got them from my parents. Both of my parents were home at night with me and my older brother. They both reminded us to do our homework and to work hard. My parents, somehow, provided my brother and me with cars to drive when we turned 16. My brother got a new car and wrecked it within a few months of driving, so he was awarded another new car. My first car was a used car, but still it was a 1986 Chevy IROC. Before I graduated, I had 3 cars. While I had the IROC, my father got a Suzuki Samari (small jeep) which I drove off and on, and then when I graduated, I received a new car. All of that sounds great doesn't it? And, I am sure this matches up with a lot of other men's childhood stories. But, does this make my father a great father? Does it make him a bad father? The answer to both of these questions are no. Now, I am not saying that my father was a terrible father at all. I think my father was and still is a good father. He treated me fairly. He punished me when I screwed up and I did my share of that. So, what was missing from making him a great father? The missing ingredients are the same things missing from the legal definition of father.

Fast forward some 20 years later or so, I was given the opportunity to be a mentor of men through our church, Browns Bridge Church in Cumming, GA. To be a mentor for the church, I had to complete a 10-11 week training which was basically like going through the material as though I was being mentored. For part of that training, I had to go back into my childhood and discuss how my parents were, how I was raised, how they loved me, what I got from them and what I didn't get from them. When it comes to my father, I know he loves me and always has. I knew he worked really hard to provide for us. He was always looking for a better opportunity so we could have more.

However, what I discovered going back into my childhood as a grown man and a father of two (2) boys myself, I realized that it was the latter part of what he was trying to do that is also the missing link for me. See, he wanted to give us more. More what? If I sat him down and asked him, he would say more stuff, more money, better house, and the list would go on and on with material types of things. The reality of what I was missing, I discovered by going through the training, was I wanted more of him. Simply put, I wanted more of my father.

There are many types of fathers. They can be absent, abusive, workaholic, and emotionally detached. The difference between workaholic and absent is a workaholic still makes it home, but the absent father is one who isn't in your life for some reason. We all know what an abusive father means. He is a man who needs to have control over us and it can be verbal abuse or physical abuse. The emotionally detached father is a man who is home, in our lives, but just doesn't seem to attach to his kids. This is very common of fathers in their 60's and 70's today. They worked, the mom stayed home. The dad provided outside, the mom provided inside. Moms raised kids and changed diapers while dads raised money and careers. This is what I discovered as a man entering my 40's.

As good as my father was to us, he just seemed emotionally detached and maybe not all the time either, but for the most part. He would work, come home and want his TV and beer. On the weekends, he worked, and then would work in the yard. If my brother or I tried to help as kids, we were sent back in the house. Being in the yard was his time and not for us to bother. Listen, I love my father with everything I got. I wouldn't trade him for another one. See, GOD gives us the perfect parents for our stories

He has planned for us. He also gave us to our parents as their perfect children for their stories. It doesn't matter what type of parents or children we are, but we are parents and children from GOD. Does this mean we get a free pass? No. Does it mean we should think of ourselves as being perfect fathers? No. It means we need to work hard at being the fathers GOD intended for us to be; and, that is no easy task.

Men are challenged all the time. Men are tempted all the time. How are we challenged and tempted? We are challenged with our wives, our kids, our jobs, and by ourselves. We are tempted with our wives, our kids, our jobs and by ourselves. Take a father who is trying to make a career for himself and his family. He is challenged with the work/family balance that we all hear about. He is challenged by his wife to be home more, do more around the house and to help handle the children. He is challenged by himself because he wants to be the best at what he does. Take that same man when he is tempted. He is tempted while working to build a career by other career opportunities that will pay him more money, more fame, and more distinction because of a title. He is tempted by his kids because when they act out, he is tempted to lay the smack down before loving them. He is tempted in his relationship with his wife because he is always working and there seems to be little time for intimacy or quality time. Do you see the cycle we fall into as men and fathers? How do we break the cycle? We have to work. We have to bring in the money to pay the bills. We have to do what we can to get ahead so we can build a future for our families. We have to control the future. All of this leads to a father being emotionally detached, a workaholic, or sometimes abusive. Can we change the pattern? Can we still do the things we need to do for our families and still be a great father? Absolutely, however, it takes a change in priorities.

I am going to tell you my story as a man and father. I got my first job in architecture in 1993. I got hired by a great firm in

Memphis and worked there for 5 years or so. During my time there, I was able to work hard and move up the ladder a little bit, but hit a ceiling and I wanted more. I started dating my wife in 1993 also. Our relationship started slow and picked up steam before we had dated a year. I knew I wanted to spend the rest of my life with her. My wife and I were married in 1994, built our first house in 1995 and had our first son, Brady, in 1996. When we got married, I was 22 years old. I started out with the get fast and furious attitude. In 1998, I moved my wife and young son to Denver, Colorado trying to advance my career. While in Denver, I was able to do exactly that, advance my career in architecture. I worked with one architectural firm and one structural engineering firm learning everything I could about residential design and construction. In 1999, I launched my own design firm, just a one-person shop. I landed many custom builders as clients and my career was going up. In 2000, we had our second son, Will. At this time, I had been married for almost 6 years, had two (2) beautiful kids and a great wife who supported me working on my career. In 2002 after the 9/11 tragedy, the company wasn't doing well, the custom market was very slow, so I started looking for opportunities with other firms.

In 2003, we moved to Tampa, FL to chase a career opportunity. At the end of 2003, I found myself laid off with no job. The very next day, a firm in Denver that had previously offered me a position, called and hired me on the spot. In January of 2004, we were back in Denver, I was working to climb the ladder and advance my career again. In June of 2005, something changed again.

Brady, our oldest son, suffered a massive stroke and his life was changed forever. Yes, our lives changed too. You can read all about that struggle in my first book, *Through a Dad's Eyes, Searching for Answers, Finding GOD*. While trying to deal with his recovery, I attempted to get back to work but something was a little different. I wasn't into my job, sort of speaking. I mean, I wanted to continue to be the great employee and everything but in the back of my mind, I knew my wife was doing all the heavy lifting for our kids, but I still didn't seem to change.

In January of 2006, I took another position with a top 10 national home builder in Atlanta, GA. Over the next 7 years, I worked my tail off to climb the corporate ladder which I did very successfully.

However, I did it at the expense of my wife and kids as I turned away from them and turned to the career as a way to cope with our son's stroke. However, as I continued to get closer to GOD, I could feel Him tugging on me to change my priorities.

But, I ignored Him and kept going.

In January of 2013, I was diagnosed with malignant Melanoma. I had the required surgery and made it through the recovery. This is when "it" hit me the hardest. I spent several months reflecting on how I may not be here for my kids. How much time did I have? What have I taught them? How have I loved them? I tell people this was GOD hitting me with a 2x4 and waking me up. I had been chasing the wrong things for way too long. I had been chasing money and titles first rather than my wife and kids. After 7 years or working hard, I gave it all up and walked away from the corporate world and successful career. I was about to turn 41 when I did this and I had no real backup plan other than I was changing my priorities. As always, I had the support of my wife during this time, but it was the support from her that helped me realize I had not been supporting her. I had been taking from her for years, but not giving back to her in the same way, the same was true of my 2 boys.

What used to be first was now last on my priority list. Yes, I am telling you that I put my career last. Before 2013, my priority list looked something like this; GOD/career tied for first place. My hobbies or interest second and my family third or last. Since 2013, my priority list looks like this GOD, my wife, my kids, my other interests like serving the church, then my career. Life has never been better! Being a great father has become my focus. Being a

Page 128

great husband is just as important. Serving my church is important. Earning peoples trust through my business is important. Earning money is needed but I no longer live for the love of money like I did before. I have discovered that if I love others before myself, humble myself to be a servant of others, and to build relationships first, then the financial reward will show up in some form. The words or actions that once were missing from my definition of a father are now part of my definition for me as a man. Love, serve, teach, coach, and mentor are more important than the legal rights or obligations, by definition, that I have with my kids.

Another way to look at it is I simply decided to give into the tug of GOD, give in to His plans for me, learn I control nothing other than my attitude, and to be the man He designed me to be, **By Design.** Am I a better father because I quit a lucrative job? Not sure. Am I a better father today than before? Probably. But, am I a great father? Probably not, but I am making it one of my priorities with the changes I have made in my life and how I live it. I am continually striving to be a great father and you can too.

Prioritize the parts of your life that mean the most. When you think about that statement, you will see what moves to the top and what moves to the bottom.

Tommy Jones doesn't claim to be a great father; however, he strives to be the best father he can to his two sons, Brady (19) and Will (16). While working on his fathering skills, he also works to be a great husband to his wife of over 21 years, Beth. Not leaving any family members out, Tommy also tries to balance time with their two Goldendoodles.

Originally from Shreveport, Louisiana, Tommy's family moved a bit as he was growing up. Eventually, he landed in Memphis, Tennessee where he graduated from high school and later college. After college, Tommy started into his career in architecture and 23 years later, resides in Cumming, GA. He has always had a passion for house design and construction.

However, as he began to reprioritize his life in 2013, Tommy found several other interests. Today, he is a published author for his story about his son's stroke. *Through a Dad's Eyes, Searching for Answers, Finding God* is a labor of love. The book tells a story from the view of Tommy and how he witnessed life for over 8 years. He currently is a mentor of men within his church, serves as a co-captain on a host team at church, serves as the president of the high school football booster club and is the CEO of Gordon-Thomas Design Group, LLC.

simple
innovative
design
GORDON
THOMAS

Tommy finds peace and joy within his faith, his relationship with God and his relationship with his family and friends.

Chapter 18

DEATH, How Do I Cope with It?
By Doug Lauffer

D. Deal with it.

E. End Stage Illness Is.

A. Ask, why?

T. Talk to God, talk to each other and talk it out with whomever WILL LISTEN.

H. Have help, have hope, live!   Help! Hope! Live!

In many ways, I have a fairy tale life. I was born to poor but, so much in love parents. They taught me to be an open person, a sponge of discovery. By the way, they did not stay poor.

Married my childhood sweetheart, Vicki Lynne Reynolds, she did not say NO and married me! We have had 45 anniversaries. We have four children, whom we adore and cherish as well as their life partners. And, now we have five (5) healthy and happy grandchildren; indeed we are blessed.

Stand-out athlete and scholar at Norwin High School, North Huntingdon, Pennsylvania who went on to have his DREAM JOB.

As an original Indiana Jones and MacGyver, Vicki and I were pioneer missionaries in Sénégal North West Africa. There, we "camped out" professionally for almost two (2) years. During those years we did CULTURAL ANTHROPOLOGY, APPLIED LINGUISTICS, and TRANSLATION; we also had a medical dispensary.

Every day was an adventure with "My Tarzan", Vicki. I felt like I was Vicki's "Jane"; she is an amazing colleague so freaking resilient, athletic and a brilliant scholar. I got to and I get to live with her every day! Yes, indeed, I live a fairy tale life! But I also deal with death.

D. Deal with it.

Our third child, Brent, was born in the African Bush. From his birth, I noticed, Brent struggled. Brent was struggling with pain. Brent has struggled with PAIN his whole life! Brent has always been a stand-out athlete, intellectual and very artistic. After many, many physician consultations, by the time Brent was 18, mom, Vicki, was calling this PAIN symptom "Brent's Mystery Pains".

Brent dealt with it. That is until he was 19; that was when he hemorrhaged. He had a geo-bleed (inside his stomach). A few weeks later we would learn this came from his CONGENITAL disease. Brent has congenital hepatic fibrosis, cirrhosis from birth. (This is a chronic progressive disease of the liver characterized by the replacement of healthy cells with scar tissue.) Brent was born with this incurable disease.

E. End stage illness is. If you know anybody with an end-stage illness it basically means waiting. Waiting to die is what end-stage means; UNLESS, you are healed. I believe in healing. Healing comes through a miracle of God. Healing can also happen by self-determination to help yourself. Healing comes through medicine. Healing happens. In Brent's case, we are waiting for him to be healed while he battles. Brent battles an end-stage disease. IN PAIN Brent has battled so long, so hard, so courageously!

In addition to needing a LIVER TRANSPLANT, Brent also now NEEDS A KIDNEY TRANSPLANT!

A. Ask why? Thousands of times I have asked why. Why does my son have this extremely rare disease disorder of the liver? Was it because his mother and I lived in Africa and had diseases of the liver? That seems obvious, doesn't it? I had malaria, hepatitis, parasites and God only knows what. But, no diagnostic team has ever put that on me. But, I ASK WHY?

Why would a boy that was so happy, have to suffer like this? Brent was seemingly healthy. He was growing up to have an exciting future of great potential.

Well, I just learned to cope; I deal with it; Brent deals with it. His mother, Vicki, and Brent's siblings and all of our family and friends deal with it. But, WHY, what is the answer? Why God? Why Doctor? Why, why, why? I don't know why but asking why seems to help me.

T. Talk. Talking things out with Vicki and the doctors and my family and friends is positive. They always help me so that I feel that I can better help my son. They clarify the reality of what is happening and what it is that I should do. Also, I discover what I can do and what I cannot do.

Saint Valentine's best quote for me is, "… Listen…" No wonder he is known for love! Listening is so wonderful and loving. People listen to me when I talk. Thank God they listen! Perhaps it is because everything about Brent's disease is so unknowable and mysterious. Brent is on a North American Rare Disease Disorder List. It is so rare and so deadly that the list is not very long at all.

Thank you for letting me 'talk' in my chapter and thank you for listening/reading.

H. Have help. Have Hope. Live.

Recently, I was crying about my son and the fatality and seemingly bleak future and the person "listening" suddenly stopped me. "DOUG, STOP IT! YOU NEED TO BE STRONG FOR HIM, FOR BRENT!"

I did stop and I said, "Thank you, you're right!" That night, I renewed my commitment to be strong; to have hope. I hope that I am doing everything that I can to **HELP** my son to live. I want to daily demonstrate my HOPE. LIVE. I am going to live and I want Brent to live the best he can while he is waiting. Waiting to be listed, waiting to be transplanted, waiting to overcome organ rejection and waiting to BE WELL; I am facing DEATH the best that I can.

Here, below, I share my son's words. Brent's story comes from his fund raising website. You will see what a great young man he is!

Brent Writes, "Dear Family and Friends,

I am writing about my need for a liver and kidney transplants.

In 1978 I was born. When I was a teen we found out that I have a liver condition, Congenital Hepatic Fibrosis. Since then, I've struggled with it. In January of 1999, surgeons in Pittsburgh performed a splenorenal shunt procedure to take care of my esophageal bleeding. The Cleveland Clinic Transplant Center is now following me.

As I struggle with liver and kidney failure, I have tried to keep a positive and hopeful attitude despite feeling ill most of the time. By God's grace I finished my college education at Community College Beaver County, PA and Thomas Edison College in New Jersey. I had a great career as a dock manager with FedEx for several years.

Unfortunately, I have been unable to work for the last few years. This past year, my condition has significantly deteriorated. Currently, I am under the care of the physicians at the Cleveland Clinic Transplant Center. Because of the severity of my condition the doctors have determined that I need a liver transplant and also now I might need a kidney. In order for me to be eligible for the transplant in the near future, I am in need of a cadaver donor. I pray someone will want to be a part of this lifesaving donation. In the meantime, I am receiving weekly albumin infusions to help relieve my severe swelling and edema.

Your prayers are greatly appreciated and will help me survive this unbelievable challenge. I want to return to a productive life as soon as possible.

With much love and appreciation, Brent Lauffer"

His website is at the following web address.
https://m.helphopelive.org/campaign/5201

Besides the reality of mortality, as a father, I have daily life-changing experiences. The drama of daily life, of dealing with the daily events of my life gives me the opportunity to be become a better person/father. The constant challenges mean constant change. Here, I try to learn each day, that is to say be a life-long learner. I have the opportunity to experience miracles every day.

To me, learning means change. The change means to become more and to become better.

Now, if I am studying something, I will change. I should become more and better in that subject matter. I am constantly thinking about and study fatherhood. Even though now I have five grandchildren, I am still learning about fatherhood and grand-fatherhood.

Fatherhood is one of those life-long learning subjects for me. Lifelong learning therefore means changing all of the time. Becoming, becoming MORE and BETTER; enjoying life, lifelong learning and life-long CHANGE.

Now, there are some quotes that have changed my life

These quotes are changing my life.

These quotes continue to change my life. I am becoming more; I'm becoming better because of these quotes. I deal with and live life better because of them.

Douglas, lad, O to Have the Gift to See Yourself as Others See You! T'would from many a blunder and foolish notion free-YA.

My grandfather, Thomas M. Miller was born and raised in Goven, Scotland. Grandfather Miller came to America and settled here as a young man. He was a draftsman for the Westinghouse Electric Corporation. As he said this to me many times throughout my childhood, I have never forgotten it. But, sometimes I forget to apply it; I'm doing better.

Keep The BEST and Leave the Rest! "In all trials and tribulations your family and your God will be your best relations."

These combined quotes come from my brother, Clarke, and from my son, Ken Lauffer.

Clarke said to me many years ago, "Keep the BEST and leave the rest!"

Life is filled many and varied opinions, ideas and quarrels. Clarke said this to me in the context of a quarrel that I was having with a colleague. Now, I try to glean something from everybody and their philosophies.

As I travel through this life, it is a continuous contemplative sojourn, I have encountered and I am encountering and I will encounter many troublesome things. I have many trials and tribulations and in each one I often and always remember my son, Ken's quote; I go to my family and to my God for the strength that I need to see me through each day's tribulations! :-)

Call Your Mother!

The fourth quote that has and is and will continue to change my life (so that I am more and a better person) comes from my father-in-law, of blessed memory, Bernard Reynolds.

Bernie once said, "Call your mother!"

Now, there is hardly a day that goes past, in the seventh decade of my life, that I do not call my mother. As a result I feel closer to Sheila more now than ever.

Each conversation we have together, I cherish. As I listen to my mother, our chats make me feel very close to her. I try to listen deeply to my mother.

I have renewed and rededicated myself to be more cautious to be more hopeful to be a better listener. "Listen." –Saint Valentine

Take heed. Be aware. Be mindful. Think.

As I consider my life:

- I have a marriage of over 45 years.
- I have four wonderful children who have accomplished so much, each one of them have done and are doing so many wonderful things in their lives for themselves, their family and God.
- Vicki and I now have five precious grandchildren, each so special and enjoying the "NOW" of their lives, proving that they too will be happy!
- Now, at 62, I feel that I have not yet arrived at total actualization and finished my race… but, I can see the goal; it will be achieved. By this, I mean that by The Grace of God, I have been, I am being and with The Help of Almighty God, I will finish my race someday; I am satisfied that I have and I am and I am at peace that I gave, give, will give MY ALL!

Permit me to end with this, I AM A MAN! I like me, and I am worthy to be a father and a grandfather. YOU ARE TOO! ☺

Why? It is because I AM; I am a human being. I try to; serve others; it is what I do—and I will forever serve by the grace and love of my Lord Jesus Christ! ☺ YOU CAN TOO!

Doug Lauffer is a minister, entrepreneur and professor at Community College Beaver County, Monaca, Pennsylvania. Professor Lauffer teaches Information Technology and Philosophy. Ordained in 1976, he has served churches in Pennsylvania, Sénégal and Uganda, Africa. His Master in Theology is from the University of Balamand; his Master of Science is from the University of Pittsburgh. He has a BA and a BSBA from Geneva College, Beaver Falls, Pennsylvania. Doug's Associate Degree is from Westmoreland County Community College, Youngwood, Pennsylvania. www.douglauffer.com

The Lauffers have four children and five grandchildren. Doug and Vicki Lauffer's third child was born in Simbandi Balant, Sénégal, Africa on December 19, 1978. They were pioneer missionaries there doing applied linguistics, cultural anthropology and translation work among the Manjak people. Son, Brent Jacques FM Lauffer was born with a congenital liver disease. Brent was in management at Federal Express. He needs a liver and kidney transplants. Brent Lauffer's fundraising website is at the following address. https://m.helphopelive.org/campaign/5201

Their other children are healthy, married with children. They have successful careers in their chosen fields. All of the kids are active in their communities and they also serve The Lord Jesus Christ in their churches.

Chapter 19

What about Cats and Dogwoods?
By Joe Walko

The white, creamy blossoms of the eastern dogwood, arranged in graceful, cascading, cantilevered layers throughout the woods, will always remind me of my father. Arguably the showiest of the spring blooming trees, the flowers of *Cornus florida* feature four petals arrayed in a cross, upturned as if giving glory to the sun, to the promise of spring, surely marking the passing of winter when they appear. They were Dad's favorite tree.

Our yard sported more than a few of them, and they were always the anchoring feature plant in Dad's landscaping designs that he worked up for clients. Landscaping wasn't his day job, but it was dad's true love. He didn't mind the hard work and back breaking physical labor necessary to complete a job. Dirt under his fingernails was a badge of honor, a marked contrast from his droll draftsman's job that paid the bills, but forced him behind a nice clean desk for too long. His passion for landscaping and building was limited to weekends and evenings, after duty.

Dad would bring me along on the jobs. He needed the help, I know now. I wasn't thrilled about giving it. Cartoons were only on Saturday mornings that far back. But I went. Dad even paid me if he was getting paid. I secretly enjoyed getting my hands in the dirt, too. But what I loved most, looking back now, was seeing a blank boring patch of green grass transform into a work of art.

Planters sprung up in the oddest places, in the oddest shapes, taking away all the corners and edges. Trees were planted strategically in the planters, large rocks and logs and other anchors were added, and small accent plants finished off the display, like the subtle notes of the musician or the sublime scenes of the writer. They made all the difference, of course. Through the smell of mulch, accompanied by birdsong, I watched the odd shapes take form, and fit perfectly together into a tapestry that I couldn't see when we started. An artist, he was painting with plants.

Dad couldn't afford to buy all of his plants at a nursery, so often times the trees we used in these jobs came from the woods. In the fall, we would traipse through the local forests, looking for small oaks and maples and white pines, and dogwoods, to be transplanted in the spring. We would tag them with brightly colored ribbon while they still had recognizable fall leaves. Now they would be easy to find in the spring, before they budded out.

Again, I wasn't thrilled to be dragged along on these forays at the time, but it gave me time in the woods with my old man. Maybe this is from where my love of the outdoors came. Certainly it is where my appreciation for dogwoods started. And most certainly planting these trees and watching them grow and bloom is where my love of landscaping and gardening and getting dirt under my nails originated, which I enjoy to this day. Thanks, Dad.

I fall back often on Dad's example of working hard, too, of working with a passion, of doing what you love, even if it is only on weekends because you have a family to take care of first. Dad didn't let obstacles and responsibilities prevent him from doing what he loved. Of course, I didn't appreciate it at the time. But I do now, as I attempt to follow my passions while still taking care of my family.

I hope to instill these values in my own children and stepchildren. It is not easy to make your way in the world today. We have too many choices; too many special interests are vying for our attention and dollar. It's hard to remember that our happiness will stem not from being given things, but from the pursuit of what is inside us, what is unique to each of us. Like making paintings, making a work of art in grass.

Sure, there will be obstacles. And yes, it will be challenging. But that is what gives our path meaning. Our blended family is not traditional by any stretch, and each of us has experienced tragedies and challenges. I want our children to know that these obstacles are not to be shied from. They shape us, are part of who we are, and provide fodder to who we can be. And they teach us lessons that only we can know.

These are hard lessons to learn, as is most of growing up. But they make us uniquely who we are, help define who we will be, and turn into gifts that are possessed only by us. "What another would have done as well as you, do not do it. What another would have said as well as you, do not say it, written as well as you, do not write it. Be faithful to that which exists nowhere but in yourself – and thus makes you indispensable", says Andre Gide.

It takes a lot of courage to follow your unique gifts and passions and curiosities, to paint your lawns. It takes a lot of guts to go out on a limb. So I want to give our children a foundation to build upon. A safe place, where they feel loved and secure. A place they can be themselves. A place they can fall back on, when they venture too far out on a limb. A place they feel secure enough to take small steps from, maybe even great leaps someday.

That's what we are attempting to build in our combined household – a place to grow courage. Courage isn't built in a vacuum. Courage takes guidance and discipline, practice, training, and hard work. These will all be encouraged at home, too. No, this isn't always easy for parents, but it is necessary to build the courage needed to live a good life.

That's what makes a house a home. Home should be a place of love and safety, where you can make mistakes and be yourself, but also a place of courage, a place to start and re-start if necessary.

Home is where this journey begins, and it is also a rest stop always available.

Yes it is scary, leaving home and embarking on your own. It is especially scary following your unique talents and creativity through the dark place they will inevitably lead. But we want our children to grow and blossom, like the dogwood on a bright spring morning. Like Dad wanted for me. That's the gift all parents want for their children.

It's not all serious, though, as my father also taught me. Even while building courage and journeying we can still enjoy the small things in life that bring joy.

Dad didn't work all the time. He shared with me his joy in simple pleasures, too. Dad loved music, and would work the loopholes of the record clubs (remember those?) to receive a dozen records for $1, promising to buy 2 more over the next two years. When the treasure chest of music arrived, he would sit around amidst the incredible jacket art, now long since lost, pouring over the lyrics and liner notes, clearly enjoying the mastery and artistry of the musicians, clearly enjoying the music.

I took it all in through osmosis. Hmm, it is still there.

I, too, love music. I love pouring over the lyrics of the bands that speak to me, I love listening to the intricate patterns of notes sewn together by true craftsmen. In pieces of passion, I can feel the heart that the musicians have put into their work. It is a labor of love, and I am lucky enough to share in it.

I still even like some of my Dad's favorite artists. He truly had an ear for good music, for some of it has stood the test of time, and still relevant.

Cat Stevens is one such artist. Dad thoroughly enjoyed Cat's art. It touched his heart, too. The songs of Cat Stevens will always make me pause and think of dad. Still today, I share the heartfelt lyrics with Dad when they unexpectedly come on the radio. I am instantly taken back to when I was a little boy, curled up in Dad's lap in front of the stereo, reading the liner notes, singing along. Back to our time together, traipsing through the woods, looking for dogwoods...

The gift from my Dad that I miss most now was just simply the time spent with him. The biggest truth is - we have limited time and resources. Dad passed away too young. He was only thirty-seven; I was only fifteen. He was sick for a couple years before he passed, too, so our time in the woods, our time doing landscaping jobs, was much too brief. Our time together was too limited; Dad's time here on Earth was just way too short. My time, our time, is limited. Use it wisely. This will always be Dad's greatest lesson.

My boys are growing rapidly, and we have two girls in the family now, too. I don't know what lessons and examples will stick with them. But I, too, am attempting to share with these children the value of hard work, and pursuing what you love with the artistry of passion, whether it is landscaping or drawing or creating music or writing, or simply working to take care of your family. I just want to see them bloom.

Enjoy the journey, kids. And make time for beauty and song, too – drink in the beauty of the springtime woods and a landscaping design, the inspiration of a song that touches your heart, and mostly, the melody of family that ties it all together.

Joe Walko is a full-time father in a non-traditional family brought together by tragedy, but blended by love. In his spare time, he is a writer and blogger searching for his voice, a seeker of his truth, a nature and adventure junkie discovering whole new worlds and beauty in the glorious struggle, in the ordinary, in his own backyard, and mostly, in his heart. Follow along at www.brokentoblended.wordpress.com and www.joewalko.wordpress.com.

Go Ask Your Dad

Chapter 20

How do you Spell Love?
By Dr. Edward L. Kropf Jr.

To be a good father, one must be humble. Being a student of your child's interests and skills is a must in the process of personal bonding and growth. Love is received in each person uniquely, especially your child. A valuable book for you to consider in the endeavor to love anyone is called *The Five Love Languages* by Gary Chapman. For now we will not consider any of these, but what I feel is the valuable underlying necessity to spelling "love" in any relationship.

I have very little knowledge in trout fishing and all that goes with it. Still, I have set aside the opening day of trout season this year to get closer to my son. This event will be shared with both my son and our fishing mentor, his father-in-law, Albert. This will be one stepping stone of many; furthering our family bonds. Together we will be out in nature doing something that has been passed on since the beginning of history. There are so many lessons in nature, each experience so unique and special. I cannot wait for this event to occur! Fathers need many resources from other men who can help in the raising of your child. Drawing from these people as a most valuable resource is an essential. I have sisters and great friends at every level; they have shared much wisdom with me. I am thankful for their impact.

Nature has always provided me with many lessons to instruct me and help me instruct others. I share these lessons with my children as well. I have accepted that we can only teach our children according to what is naturally drawing them in and what they're yearning to know. I have adopted a philosophy to lead my children **not** to the direction of my personal "house," i.e. my thinking, but to the direction of their minds. Our goal ought to help them envision their gifts and to value their inherent individualism which is unique to them. No doubt, I could answer their life's questions directly and provide a reasonable answer to them. After all, I have lived this life for many decades, right? However, that thinking assumes that we own our children! But, nothing could possibly be more incorrect. It may be easier to do it that way, but it will not raise a child. It will not help them grow.

In no way does this supersede the teachings that we must give our children in discerning right from wrong. My children have learned that there is a price to pay for poor decisions and rewards for making good decisions. That's not to say that I am the absolute judge in all facets of their deeds. I attempt to teach them the difference between home, school, work, and play. Also, I teach them the appropriateness and inappropriateness of their actions in relation to their surroundings. For example, teaching them that the languages/tones of voices that are appropriate playing with their friends outside are deemed inappropriate in school or at home. This example can be very simply extrapolated to any and all social interactions. One thing my father did teach me, "If you complain, you better have options to fix it as well." I found myself complaining as to not having the father model to emulate as a dad. I chose to read parenting books form a close by Christian book store and to the best of my ability, I've fixed it as good as I could. I've also shared with my sons that I am a better father than my father. They know that it's now their job to be a better father than I am. So I have passed this generational growth torch onto my sons with personal hope.

Having said this, my choice has been to watch and listen. We all have two ears to hear, two eyes to see, and one mouth to speak when asked. It is clear to me that, based on the proportions of sense instruments we have, we must learn to listen and watch before we speak. What I mean is we have to learn to hear with our ears what our children are saying and watch with our eyes what they do to find out what lies deep inside their hearts. Only after these important investigations can we speak into them. We even ought to learn to ask questions, which uses our one mouth to prod our children's hearts. Above all, this investment we give them, let them know they are loved.

Do my children always finish with "OH YEAH; Thanks, that's what I needed to know!" Definitely not. In time we get there. Although at times it is a spontaneous light turned on, then this is always amazing. Even then the agreements that we might share change over time. Most of the time the question and answer exchanges have to be tabled for one reason or another. However, they can resume on a later date, and fathers must initiate the continuation. Invest the time because this pays higher dividends than any bucks working over-time at your job. It will be a greater gift than any material object you could give them.

Patience a virtue as fleet and quick

When there is cold beer waiting to drink

Or a fav TV program that just can't wait

Oh, Lord what an investment mistake

As science has shown, though trillions upon trillions of snow-flakes have fallen, the matrix of individual snow-flake is incredibly unique. We'd expect them to be the same. Knowing this, I have brought this to my son's perspectives that they might seek to know themselves. There's this lie that fathers face which isolates their children. It is thinking that our children are all the same and then treating each of them the same way. Likewise I also say to you fathers, don't compare yourselves to others. Your gifts are special and unique to you. We have about 75 Trillion cells; each cell is infinitely more complex than a simple snow-flake. Why should we try to be the same as anyone else? We can't be. How can we compare our kids and force them into the mold of someone else? We shouldn't try because it's impossible. This is a simple truth.

As fathers our job is to help lay a good foundation for our children. We are *The Point Man* for our families, leading the way and seeing beyond what is seen. As a Point Man foresees potential dangers, is always on guard, and ensures safe travels of his troops, so our fathers ought to be the same *Point Men* with our children. To make use of another metaphor, we, as people, are all stones along all children's paths of life. A stone is a point of reference along a person's path of life. Each stone, with its contribution in guidance and support, influences our children's lives as a direction forever as they continue on their path in life. This could impact them either positively or negatively because there is no stone that has no or neutral impact. As a father, we're trying to our children's lives positively, and seeking to guard them, as *The Point Man*, from the negative stones that they will come across.

Each of us has interests, aptitudes, and gifts as humans. Believe me when I say, projecting your likes and dislikes onto your children with the expectation that they should agree with you is not a good thing. This creates a mixed network of mind twisting thoughts within them. If we persist in doing this to them, later on that child may run into someone else who tells them how to think. Without the background of thought process maturity, they could easily be lead into harmful situations. Our goal is not to tell them what to think, but to teach them how to think. Many parents, naïve or prideful, think they know what their child's direction should be. To a certain extent, telling them is simply not your job. It may be easier to do it that way, but when has the easy road proven the better road? Find in your child the shear uniqueness that embodies their very essence. We cannot make up their minds for them. We can only try to help them find their unique directions and answers. The hard path is to listen to them and prod them with the deeper questions to get them thinking about what their saying themselves. Again, the best thing we can do listen with two ears, watch with two eyes and talk as if our mouths were glued shut. Just try to get on their level as they discuss with us their passions, desires, and interests, while constantly monitoring them without their knowledge.

May wisdom be on my lips and speak through them to my child. A smart person can learn from his/her own mistakes, but a wise person can learn from other's mistakes so that he/she doesn't have to make them himself/herself. Teach your child first to acknowledge his/her own mistakes, then to how to learn from them. After this, how to learn from the mistakes of others, so that they don't have to make them After all, we simply don't have enough time to make all the mistakes and learn from them ourselves.

Be humble enough to remind your child that you are human! Do this as early as possible. Instill in their minds that you're not perfect; and that you're not the alpha and the omega of their lives. Also, be humble enough to seek good mentors! Seek wise council from trusted men and women in decision making. Just know that they may have opinions that may not be correct. Children will watch earnestly while you ask for others opinions. They will watch as you seek and wrestle with all the information that you find. Share this process with your child, they will surely need it. Listening and asking for counsel is a life-long skill.

One I shared with my oldest happened in grad school. I learned this after receiving a 58% on a test during my first trimester. I about died as I had never studied so hard in my life. Knowing this class fails students an average of 30% each semester, I felt doomed! Exhausted from the pace of study and the failed test score, I went to the president of the school, Dr. Janse, who was a close personal friend of my dad. I asked for him to help me obtain a tuition refund in order to quit. He told that it simply wasn't in the university's policy to do so. Whether that is true or not, Dr Janse saw right through the problem and sent me to seek council. Dr. Janse then sent me to have a meeting with Dr. Christenson who had given the test that I failed. Dr. C sat me down, explained the class average on that test was 56% and began reviewing with me the first 5 questions. As he asked each question I provided a short dissertation on what I could recall. Dr. C smiled, spoke softly, removing the ornate pipe from between his lips and said; "Ed you certainly have a good grasp of each of the 5 test questions, although you did get them all wrong!" Immediately I branded myself with the mark of "test-taking failure." Dr. C encouraged me, asking me to take a blank piece of paper and cover the multiple choice answers. He told me that after reading and understanding the question, I should seek the most correct of the 5 answers. His testing style was similar to how he instructed, which couldn't be learned from a book. This experience made me wish I was humble enough to sit and chat with him on the 1st day of class (I later took up this practice). Dr. C was also kind enough to impart to me this wisdom; "study less hours and take great notes." I used this and went to a girl from the class to get a copy of her notes. I followed this wisdom to a "T." On the next test I scored the 2nd highest grade in the class with an 88%! May your children be blessed with great mentors!

One time, when my son was having studying and test-taking problems, I imparted to him all of the wisdom I had learned from this experience. He took it in and after a bit of a fight to learn new habits, he now enjoys a greater than 3.9 GPA! I kept feeding him the smart things I learned; "study ahead, learn word meanings, ask the professor early about what the learning objectives are, get good sleep, read and reread your written work, etc…" in hopes that he would become wise. My son might not have listened to me if I hadn't shared embarrassing educational moments with him. Be humble! Later we talked about many of my screw ups and I assured him, I admit them all for the height of true wisdom. He listened.

Importantly, you must be there for them. Be solid, so you don't go into self-pity and feel like your children are using you, though it may really feel that way. It's not about you! It's about forming and keeping a relationship with your child. I have practiced these things since my children's early years. I attempt to reach my children in many different ways. This has helped me greatly as they are now young men and see me as the imperfect man I am, choosing to love me. This underlying foundation to your relationship protects the bond against the falsity of perfectionism. If that false standard of unattainable perfection is there, then this would eventually result in losing the relationship altogether. Humility, not pride, will drive you to this.

As fertilizers of life to my child's care

The life's lessons I humbly submit to share

May our children's wisdom grow indeed

As we bond closer, yes, my children and me.

"How does a child spell love? T-I-M-E!" Zig Ziglar exclaimed. I LOVE that! It embodies the best that I can do as a dad. Not having a father as an example myself, I learned from some friends' fathers and read many books. A few things I have learned through the following years, Time isn't just quantity. Time should be regularly available with some openness and real interest in your child. They are as unique and special as Christmas gifts. The children are unwrapped! It's our job to help them un-wrap the special, unique, and wonderful spirit within them.

In conclusion, be on the look-out for those blessed times when you can accomplish some miraculous progress in finding your child's future direction. Don't blow it with the "something came up" excuse, humility has told me. Children are a father's gift. I choose to invest in them my most precious asset I have. It is the only thing I can NOT get back; my *time*! Investing in your children pays better dividends than any other investment! So, I will invest the opening day of trout fishing with my son. I will choose to foster our relationship by sharing in an interest he has. I like to play golf, but my son doesn't.

We fish. It's my choice to see it as it is; time with him.

Prepare your child for the road ahead
Not the road ahead for your child
Yes at time peace will fill their hearts
And at others, hearts running wild
The road has hills, both up and down
With twists turns and bends
Be that rock in your child's life's path
To seek direction, refuge and mend.
When trouble breaks their bones or spirit be
A curator of each and every need
Find understanding from your honest healed past
You'll find what was missing in raising me.

Edward L Kropf Jr. is a Pittsburgh Pa. based third generation Chiropractic Physician. His grandfather also maintained an Osteopathic degree and studied herbal medicine in Europe. His father a Chiropractor and was recognized as an expert in x-ray interpretation. Doc Jr. Post-graduate degrees and interest are: Integrated Medicine, Functional Medicine, Wellness, and Concussions as related to accidents and sports. He has taught technique and provides wellness and health talks including anti-aging to groups, communities, organizations and professionals.

To date Doc's proudest accomplishment and passion involved raising and being a stepping stone in his sons' lives, current ages 21 and 20. He loves his children very much indeed. Not experiencing a close time/activity relationship with his own father, Doc took up the cross, listened and learned by great wisdoms in books and by others examples and spent every moment available sharing with his children. Long woods walks or asphalt jungle excursions made available opportunities to invoke life lesson wisdom into his boys.

Doc enjoys a healthy relationship with Jesus as his personal mentor.

Go Ask Your Dad

Chapter 21

What is Normal Anyway?
By Dennis Newton

I remember sobbing on the floor uncontrollably, my eyes were so heavy and I couldn't even lift my body off the floor to go to bed. It wasn't late or even bed time. I was simply drained, drained of emotional, mental and physical energy. I was immobile and my mind was like an amusement park ride that spins around and the floor drops out. I was that one person that pukes without fail. My daughter pulls me by the arm, looking at me sympathetically, imploring me to "just go to bed". The dishes and laundry and things that need to be done can wait, right now you need to go to bed. I think it was 6:30 p.m.

It's not that doing dishes and laundry and meal planning and all the things that go into running a household aren't so draining or taxing, although as a single parent those tasks sometimes seem daunting. Over time you learn to adjust and find yourself being quite efficient. You will even catch yourself snickering at parents in a so-called normal home when they tell their heroic tales of getting kids to sports practices and parent teacher conferences. In the midst of running here and there and all the while managing to binge watch their favorite show on Netflix snuggly fit into their schedule. What I experienced had nothing to do with the details of day to day but everything to do with the thief of all joy, comparison. We all compare our life to others and we all experience loss of joy at some point in our lives. Nothing zaps a man's strength faster than feeling inadequate, looking around and seeing your kid's friends with nicer clothes or the latest mobile device. We can easily make peace with our kids perhaps not having the latest and greatest, but the one comparison I found myself so addled by was the divorce and single parent status.

To begin with, it seemed like all my kid's friends had perfect intact families and my kids were stuck with just dad. Not to mention, all of my friends were successful and happily married. I couldn't attend sporting events or school functions like I wanted to, or fit in helping on a science fair project. I couldn't do any of this all the while cooking dinner and trying not to think about the work day looming in seemingly a few short hours after an abbreviated night's sleep. These activities and tasks do not have the power to beat any parent down; after all we are all busy these days. Busy and distracted, but that is a whole new topic we won't discuss to the time being. There are enough stresses and duties to tend to on a daily basis for any person or parent let alone a single parent. The last thing any of us needs is to talk ourselves into believing we are failing our kids.

If you are reading this book right now chances are you take parenting seriously, as an honor that has been placed before you.

I was recently listening to a recording of one of my favorite mentors, she said, "We believe twenty percent of what others say about us and eighty percent of what we say about ourselves." I am not talking about what we say openly. I am talking about when you are acting as if you have everything under control and you are smiling or being super-dad. Yeah, I got this and No, I'm good and I do not require any assistance whatsoever. You know the persona we try to convince our peers of or maybe we are just trying to convince ourselves. The self-talk nobody hears, well hopefully nobody hears. Could you imagine sitting at your desk at work voicing your inner thoughts. I think I know a few people who do! It is not pretty how we treat ourselves sometimes. I know I can be my own worst critic instead of looking at my own self-reflection.

Self-reflection is a good thing. Studies show that seventy seven percent of our self-talk is negative, well isn't that encouraging! At least it is encouraging to know we are not alone. From my experience, in times of heightened emotions, is when that seventy seven percent seems like seven hundred and seventy seven and when you are raising three teenage children by yourself heightened emotions occur nonstop. It's during these times when you can forget about the twenty three percent you used to rely on to get through the day with a smile on your face and the energy in reserve to do something for yourself such as brush your teeth before bed or read a book for a few minutes.

It is in these times when you forget you have people in your community who are pulling for you and friends and family you can call or text for advice, encouragement and support. It is when you forget that you have a plan. Being a single dad with a teenage daughter caused me to plan purposely to surround her with women I admire. Women she could mimic and emulate their character. I am forever grateful to the women who have participated in assisting me in shaping my daughter to be a woman who is full of character and dignity and believes in herself. And when that teenage daughter is a bundle of raw emotions and with the energy to fuel a raging volcano, any man can forget he has a plan. This is when the seventy seven percent takes over and says, "Oh my gosh I'm failing at this, I can't do this or maybe she is better off living with her mother and not with three boys who wrestle and choke people out for a pastime."

These thoughts and feelings are what cause you to collapse in a heap at 6:30 p.m. on a Tuesday night with your daughter tugging on your arm imploring you to go to bed. I did go to bed that night at 6:30 p.m. I may have slept in my clothes for all I remember. I do not know if the kids had dinner that night or if they stayed up all night eating pop tarts and playing X-box. I wish I could say something really inspiring, like after that night, I learned the secret to never becoming overcome with exhaustion or I magically had only feelings of euphoria and always felt I am the greatest parent since the dad from Leave it to Beaver or maybe My Three Sons.

Parenting is not always going to be like a television show. Sometimes it does feel like a struggle, and in those times I focus on the twenty three percent. In reality I remember I do have a plan and I am more closely connected with my kids than I ever was when I was married to their mother. You know when everything was "normal".

The truth is there is no normal, the experience we are having as a family is both unique to us and similar to so many all at the same time. It is our experience and it is perfect for us and full of love and support and learning and growing. In the beginning of this past school year I adopted the following mantra, "This is fun, this is easy and I am having the time of my life." I consider this mantra a substantial upgrade over the previous school year when I adopted "see me in a fight with a bear, please pray for the bear." The night I staggered to bed at 6:30 p.m. I felt like the bear had won.

Please pray for me because the bear just thrashed me. Sometimes the bear does win and it is okay. I have learned now not to compare our story to any other family. I mean I can draw inspiration or a great idea from another dad or family and add their wisdom to my tool bag.

However, I do not look at other families and compare results or things or even experiences. This is our experience and it is perfect for us. I no longer allow my joy to be stolen by comparison, instead I choose to thoroughly soak in and enjoy every moment with my kids resting peacefully knowing all is well, perfect and good. I would not trade what we have for all the normal in this world.

Dennis Newton currently lives in Plum Borough a suburb of Pittsburgh, Pennsylvania. After suddenly being thrust into single parenthood in 2012 he had a choice to make; get better and see this event as an opportunity for growth or, as a setback to all his hopes and dreams. With much consideration and after licking his wounds, Dennis began the beautiful process of planning and designing his life as a single dad. Dennis approached it with a sense of wonder and excitement. The results have been an incredibly close relationship with his children and a renewed sense of purpose.

Dennis states, "We may not choose everything that happens in our life but we do choose how to react. I have chosen to become #singledadwithaplan and I desire to inspire other parents to choose to embrace their super hero hidden inside of them." **Dennis Newton** also enjoys spending time with his kids, taking long walks with the dog, playing ultimate Frisbee and volunteering at Amplify Church in Plum, Pennsylvania.

Go Ask Your Dad

Chapter 22

Who Do You Want To Be?
By Darnell Johnson

The year was 1992; I was seventeen years of age and she was sixteen years of age and we had no idea what life had in store for us. When I say, she, I'm referring to my oldest daughter's mother. Her name is Theresa and we met at Greater Works Christian Academy located in Murrysville PA, maybe fifteen or twenty minutes outside of Pittsburgh, home of the greatest NFL franchise in the world the Pittsburgh Steelers. I started going to Greater Works Academy in 1989 when I was in the 8th grade and I stayed until the end of my tenth grade year. My whole eighth grade year I had my eyes on this super cute female who I liked but never really had the heart to tell her. We were signing yearbooks at the end of the year so I finally gathered the heart to sign her yearbook and tell her how I felt. Well to shorten the story, let's just say that my eighth grade crush became my ninth grade girlfriend. I was fifteen when our relationship left the friend zone so by the time I reached sixteen I truly believed I was in love.

In 1992 I was entering the tenth grade and I'm coming off a summer of experiences that naturally had me feeling or should I say smelling myself a little bit. I still believed I was in love with Theresa but the dynamic of me smelling myself was having a profound effect on how I dealt with other females. My tenth grade year of high school I actually had four different girlfriends but my heart was always with Theresa. Being an immature teenage boy my ability to express my feelings with any degree of confidence was limited. On the outside it just looked like I was running around trying to impersonate some kind of player but in all actuality I had to succumb to the natural pressures of being a teenage boy in high school. At some point in my tenth grade year Theresa and I decided it was time to take our relationship to the next level and for that reason sex was imminent.

Well, we ended up having sex and approximately two weeks later she came to the school and told me she was pregnant. Now at the time I'm sixteen with three other females that I'm dealing with in the same school. I really wasn't informed on a timetable perspective on how long it takes for a female to know she is pregnant but, I definitely felt that two weeks wasn't enough time. I not only accused her of lying about the pregnancy but once the pregnancy was confirmed I denied the possibility of the baby being mine. At the time I felt like everything was happening so fast it became a little overwhelming so on cue I decided to deny and run.

Well that thought process was short-lived and I dove in head first into the responsible fatherhood thing. I got a job and became attached to Theresa all over again. I remember looking at her at times thinking she was the prettiest pregnant female in the world and we really are about to be a family. Looking back I think the pregnancy drew me closer to her emotionally, but she seemed to become more and more emotionally detached from me.

When my daughter was born I didn't want to be anywhere else but with Theresa and my daughter. I wasn't dealing with any other females. At that point, I honestly believed we were going to be a family for life. I was seventeen and Theresa was sixteen and we were from opposite ends of the spectrum. Theresa was from the south side of Pittsburgh where the neighborhood was more suburban and much more diverse. She had attended to Greater Works Academy since kindergarten. Greater Works is a private school so from a worldly experience and stand-point she was extremely limited in her knowledge of the world. I was from a housing development called East Hills located on the eastside of the city of

Pittsburgh. I don't think I need to go into too much detail about my neighborhood, but by the time my daughter was born I had seen death first hand by way of gang violence as well as heavy drug traffic.

Drugs affected my household as well as the 75% of the households in my neighborhood. Since Theresa was pregnant, she had to go to an alternative school along with other pregnant females as well as guys who had gotten into trouble in their regular schools and needed to make up credits. To shorten this story while going to alternative school Theresa would naturally come to meet new people, other influences both male and female. Theresa ended up meeting another guy so consequently she and I grew further and further apart. She was no longer interested in being in a relationship with me. To say I was heartbroken would be a grave understatement. I responded to this reality in the worst possible way. I became so angry at Theresa for not wanting to be with me anymore that I began to take it out on my daughter.

Although I truly loved my daughter I knew this was the only card I had to play to get back at Theresa for hurting me. I started to neglect my responsibilities as a father in the worst ways. I became the typical young father that failed to step up and handle the circumstances that he created for himself. I wasn't spending any real quality time with my daughter and I allowed myself to become desensitized to the whole thought of being a stand up dad. I allowed my hurt feelings towards Theresa to negatively influence my decision making as a young father and my daughter ultimately paid the price for that. In the midst of all this running from responsibility I was creating more responsibilities for myself.

I met a beautiful young lady named Lovey and began to have a physical relationship with her that was short lived but the picture we painted was beautiful. Lovey got pregnant and had a son who she named Darnell after his dad. Lovey died from heart complications when Darnell was six months old. Here I am a young nineteen year old immature boy with two children; I have no idea of my level of influence in their lives. My oldest daughter was born in 1992, my middle child my son was born two years later in 1994. Yea, you guessed it; in 1996 my baby girl was born. In the year 1997 I found myself mentally and emotionally overwhelmed with the responsibility of being a father of three beautiful children as well as dealing with the dark reality of being a young black male in the impoverished inner city.

My fatherhood story takes a drastic turn for the worst when I was convicted of second degree murder and sentenced to life in prison without the possibility of parole.

Now, at the age of twenty-two I was sent to a State Correctional Institution to serve a life sentence and I have three children with whom I have yet to form any type of bond with. At this time my oldest daughter is four turning five, my son is one turning two and my baby girl is six months old approaching one full year. When I first went to prison my mom and dad were both in prison so my life was a little chaotic to say the least. Being as though I was the poster child for Dead Beat Dads my attempts to make contact with any of my children were viewed through negative eyes.

During the first two or three years of my incarceration I had to really go inside myself to find out who I was as a young man. That to me meant who I was and who did I want to be as a son, brother, uncle, and more importantly who did I want to be as a father. This wasn't a time to expect any sympathy or, even make any excuses for past mistakes and poor decision making.

This was a time for me to look into the mirror, come to grips with whom I was, acknowledge the damage that I've caused and ask myself... WHO DO YOU WANT TO BE MOVING FORWARD? Looking into that mirror I learned a lot about myself and I came away knowing and understanding that I needed to concentrate on being the absolute best man that I could possibly be. I realized that by being the best man I could be, I will also be the best son, brother, uncle and above all father that I could be as well.

My three children were all under the age of six with their entire lives ahead of them and I wanted to be a part of each of their lives intimately moving forward. I knew that when time permitted each one of my children would want to know who I was, where I was and why I wasn't home.

When these questions and similar ones were asked I wanted the opportunity to answer. I began to write letter after letter to my daughters because I really didn't know where my son was at the time. I wrote and I talked to Taylor and Maurquise about everything. I asked them their favorite colors, favorite TV shows, and foods. I asked about school, family members, and friends—pretty much everything concerning them. I wrote for about four years before getting one response. I was disappointed when I wasn't getting any responses but at the same time I was extremely grateful to even have the opportunity to write and to allow my children to have some understanding of who I am, what my thoughts are and most of all no matter what I loved them. I first had the opportunity to establish a relationship with Tayler my oldest daughter. She wrote me back for the first time when she was nine years old. Although the road hasn't always been smooth Tayler's and my relationship has blossomed and she loves me. I got the chance to see her after twelve years on her sixteenth birthday which was one of the best days of my life. Tayler was four when I first came to prison she is now twenty three and I'm blessed to have a wonderful relationship with her in spite of the time and distance between us.

Maurquise, my youngest daughter, whom I call baby girl, was six months old when I came to prison. She is now nineteen.

Ms. Helen Maurquise's great grandmother's mother, may she rest with God, she was responsible for keeping the lines of communication open between Maurquise and me. Ms. Helen and I wrote for years and she kept me informed. She sat Maurquise down and taught her how to write me letters and address the envelopes as well as sending pictures allowing me to enjoy Maurquise's maturation. I got to see Maurquise for the first time after six years when she was eight years old. In the beginning of her and me getting to know one another, Maurquise couldn't even bring herself to call me dad when we were face to face or when we were on the phone. I'm blessed to say the whole dad thing isn't an issue anymore. We literally are best friends and I think she might say Dad a little too much now. ☺

My son Little Darnell is now twenty years old and our relationship is doing well under the circumstances. Darnell is now awaiting trial in the Allegheny County Jail for robbery homicide, which are the same exact charges I faced over eighteen years ago. I acknowledge my absence played a part in Darnell's choices and I haven't had the chance to connect to him like his sisters and I have, but we know that we love one another and we are moving forward in a positive direction on the strength of that foundation. As a man I was blessed with the ability to reproduce but along with that ability come's a much greater responsibility. I had to learn that responsibility and apply it to my life and circumstances and I'm blessed to say that even though I've been in prison my children's whole lives they often tell me I'm the best Dad in the world. I know and understand where my blessings come from and I am forever thankful to God that my children gave me the second chance to be their Dad. Dad and father are just titles by themselves. Through our actions we as men have the opportunity to bring a unique definition to those titles.

The duties of a Dad doesn't change not matter what the circumstances are. You can be in another city, state, county or even incarcerated but your obligations and duties as a father don't change. No matter what the circumstances are we have to always be in the business of being the best men we can be, and in turn we will ultimately become the best fathers we can be as well. I want Tayler

Darnell and Maurquise my beautiful children to know that I love them beyond the expression of any words. A very special thanks to Mrs. Darnella Williams, Mr. Art Williams, Ms. Sherell Burks and Ms. Gina R. Johnson for being the driving force behind the lines of communication. They kept them open between my children and me and gave me a second chance at sharing their lives with them.

Darnell Johnson is a son of the wonderful Ms. Gina R, Johnson. He is the proud big brother of Jacquet Bazemore Johnson and Robert Lawson Johnson and he's an equally proud little brother to the late Mr. Ricardo Johnson (RIP). Darnell is also the proud uncle of ten nieces and nephews and one great niece Ms. Ny'Siah Adams. Although he states they're a handful he is blessed to have three beautiful children Tayler, Little Darnell and Maurquise whom he loves beyond the expression of words.

Darnell claims his life is pretty much an open book and he believes anyone who chooses to read it will have an understanding of his mistakes as well as an appreciation for his growth and maturity. Mr. Johnson is currently serving a life sentence in a State Correctional Institution in Pennsylvania for second degree murder conviction.

Darnell has been incarcerated for a little over eighteen years. He states he came to prison when was a twenty one year old immature boy and now is blessed to say that he is a forty year old mature man.

Darnell is thankful that his sanity is secure after eighteen years and he is honored that now he is in the position to affect someone's life in a positive way. What comes along with being a mature man is a sense of responsibility for his actions moving forward. Also, Darnell accepts the accountability for his past actions. With him moving forward even under these circumstances Darnell realizes that he has within him the responsibility to learn and grow from mistakes as well as set some kind of positive example for others.

Darnell Johnson is the Chairman of the Lifers and Long termers Committee which is a sub-committee of the Hope For Change organization at SCI Forest. Hope For Change is a non-profit prisoner-run organization that promotes social awareness, growth, development and positive change in one's character and outlook on life while also improving the quality of life for S.C.I. Forest's population as well as giving back to the outside communities.

Darnell acknowledges the H.F.C. provides him with a huge opportunity to show that his mistakes and poor decision making in life do not define who he is as a man. As the Co-Chairman of the Lifer and Long termers Committee of the H.F.C. organization he believes, knows and understands that the sole meaning of LIFE is to serve humanity. Knowing this Darnell Johnson would rather be known for being the one who encourages others instead of the one who inadvertently hinders or discourages those around him.

Can You Do the Fatherhood Challenge?

Complete this challenge successfully and in seven days you will be on your way to becoming a better Dad!

Day One: Begin to say, "I love you" to your children and spouse and repeat everyday

Day Two: Do not discipline in anger- step back from the situation and cool down

Day Three: Do not let your children see you put anything unhealthy in your body

Day Four: Turn off the television and put down your cell phone

Day Five: Participate in an outside activity

Day Six: Enjoy a home cooked that was prepared together

Day Seven: Take accountability and solve a family concern without expecting a congratulations or reward

NOTES:

_____

_____

_____

_____

_____

Epilog

During a telephone call my sister once asked me, "Aren't you afraid when you write a book about fatherhood that people will find out you're not always perfect?" To my sister, my friends, and any other parents reading *Go Ask Your Dad*, Am I afraid; absolutely not! I'll proclaim it, I'll shout it from the top of the mountain- I am not a perfect man. I am not a perfect dad, I don't have all the answers, and as many of our authors mentioned, I am not Super Dad. What, and who I am is a man trying to be the best father, son, husband, friend, brother, writer, role-model, and employee I can be.

As fathers, all we can do is strive to be <u>our</u> best. I cannot be someone else, but I can be me, the best dad I can be. The men of this book live by this principle. Many of these men never knew or rarely felt a father's love; however they were determined to be better men and not to repeat the cycle. Not only did they not repeat the cycle, they created a new generation of children who will never know the pain they once felt. Others, like me, idolized their fathers and made it their mission to be even more impactful in their children's lives. We challenged ourselves and said if our dads were able to do this, then maybe we can accomplish more.

In *Go Ask Your Dad*, we learned that circumstance, sexual orientation, and skin color do not determine or diminish the love between a father and his children. We learned that even though there are huge challenges to being a father, it's worth the effort. We read beautiful stories about the love between daddy and daughters, and troubling tales about the absence of fatherhood. We found out the significance of having a donut with dad and also the importance of #stoppingfatherlessness. The fathers reminded us of great dads in generations past, and prepared us for greater dads yet to come. We learned that time passes too quickly, but time is often what father and child cherish most. We met polar opposites and each taught us about the importance of a father's presence. Our Dads accepted responsibility for the role they have played, and all committed to bettering their relationships.

We've offered stats, stories, answers, and tools, but what we learned is that we can't give you time. Valuable quality time between father and child is for you to create. Please accept our message and our challenges, and understand we are just imperfect fathers trying to do our best and share what we have learned, hoping to ease another family's journey. If this book helps one dad or one family, please know this, there will be twenty two fathers who accomplished their mission.

And, my mother, Sheila Lauffer, agrees with Dominick Domasky. Everybody, please, aspire to BE GREAT and to KEEP BEING AWESOME! ☺

Thank you!

Dominick Domasky and Doug Lauffer
with the Authors of *Go Ask Your Dad*